Why can't computer books be easier to understand?

Not all of us want to become computer professionals, but we do want to have fun with our computers and be productive. The new *Simple Guides* cover the popular topics in computing. More importantly, they are simple to understand. Each book in the series introduces the main features of a topic and shows you how to get the most from your PC.

Simple Guides – No gimmicks, no jargon, no fuss

Available in the *Simple Guides* series:

The Internet

Searching the Internet

The PC

Office 2000

Windows 98

E-commerce

Digital cameras, scanning and
  using images

Internet research

Building a website

Creating and using spreadsheets

Using email

Putting audio and video on your website

Writing for your website

Flash 5 for Windows

Windows Me

Windows XP

A simple guide to

Dreamweaver MX

Belinda Walthew

Prentice Hall

An imprint of PEARSON EDUCATION

Pearson Education Limited

Head Office:
Edinburgh Gate
Harlow
Essex CM20 2JE
Tel: +44 (0)1279 623623
Fax: +44 (0)1279 431059

London Office:
128 Long Acre
London WC2E 9AN
Tel: +44 (0)20 7447 2000
Fax: +44 (0)20 7447 2170
website: www.it-minds.com

Published in Great Britain in 2002
© Pearson Education Limited 2002

ISBN 0-130-45824-4

The right of Belinda Walthew to be identified
as the author of this work has been asserted by her in accordance
with the Copyright, Designs and Patents Act 1988.

British Library Cataloguing-in-Publication Data
A catalogue record for this book can be obtained from the British Library.

10 9 8 7 6 5 4 3 2 1

Typeset by Pantek Arts Ltd, Maidstone, Kent.
Printed and bound by Ashford Colour Press, Gosport, Hampshire.

The publishers' policy is to use paper manufactured from sustainable forests.

About the author

Belinda Walthew is an Australian Web skills trainer and developer based in the UK. Belinda offers customised on- and off-site training courses and can be reached at: belindawalthew@btconnect.com

Contents

Introduction . . . .*xviii*

System requirements xviii

    For a PC running Microsoft Windows xix

    For a Macintosh xix

Installing Dreamweaver xix

Keyboard and shortcut conventions xx

Panel shortcuts xx

Adopted conventions xxi

1 What's in a Website? 1

What is HTML? 2

How does a Website get on to the Internet? 3

Planning a Website 5

Understanding the site goals 5

Identifying the site audience 6

Thinking about site navigation 7

What text? 7

Which images? 8

But is it dynamic? 9

Managing the Website 9

Some useful references 10

2 Getting started in Dreamweaver 13

The Dreamweaver MX workspace 14

   The Document window 14

   The Toolbar 18

   The Status bar 19

   The Property inspector 20

   The Insert bar 20

   Panel groups 22

   Using Context menus 23

Setting up a site in Dreamweaver 24

Working with files and folders 28

Opening an existing site in Dreamweaver .29

Deleting a site from the Site window 29

Changing the look of the Site window 29

Using the Site Map 30

Printing the Site Map 31

3 Creating a basic Web page 33

Opening a page 34
Setting the Page Properties 36
Creating and formatting text 38
Paragraphs and line breaks 41
    Aligning paragraphs 41
    Inserting line breaks 41
Inserting and editing horizontal rules 42
Using special characters 43
Working with lists 44
Importing text created in Microsoft Word 45
Saving a page 46
Previewing the page in a browser 47
Printing a page 48

4 Images and links 51

Inserting an image 52
Image properties 52
Resizing an image 56
Image alignment 56
Creating links 57
    Linking from one page to another 58

Linking to another Website 59
Creating an email link 59
Linking to items within a page (anchor links) .60
Linking to an anchor in another page 62
Linking using jump menus 62
Editing jump menus 64
Linking with image maps 65
Creating a simple mouse rollover 67

5 Designing with tables 69

The Dreamweaver table tools 71
Using Layout View 71
Drawing table cells 71
Adding content to a table cell 73
Table and cell options in Page Layout 73
Changing the width of a cell or column 75
Making cells and content consistent widths 77
What is the spacer image? 77
Nesting tables 77
Creating tables in Standard View 79
Inserting a table 79
Selecting a table 79

Additional table properties 80
Working with table cells 81
Formatting individual cells 81
Working with rows and columns 82
Formatting rows and columns 83
Adding rows and columns 83
Deleting rows and columns 83
Merging and splitting cells 84
Resizing a table 85
Importing tables into Dreamweaver 85

6 Working with frames 87

Understanding frames and the frameset 89
Creating a frameset 89
Adding content to frame pages 91
Saving a frameset and frame pages 92
Formatting a frameset 92
Change the width and/or height of a frame 93
Formatting individual frames 93
Linking between pages in a frameset 95
Creating a nested frameset 96
Adding existing pages to a frameset 96
NoFrames Content: what's that? 98

7 Creating forms 99

Creating a form 101
Understanding form objects 103
Using form objects 104
  Creating a single-line text field 104
  Creating a multi-line text field 105
  Inserting a password field 105
  Inserting checkboxes 106
  Inserting radio buttons 107
  Inserting a radio button group 107
  Adding a menu 109
  Adding a list 110
  Inserting a file field 110
  Adding a hidden field 111
  Inserting form buttons 112
  Inserting an image field 112
Some useful references 113

8 Advanced formatting using styles 115

Understanding styles 116
Using HTML styles 116

Applying an HTML style 118

Removing an HTML style 119

Editing an HTML style 119

Using Cascading Style Sheets (CSS) 119

Getting to know the style options 119

Creating a Custom Style (class) 122

Applying a Custom Style 122

Removing a Custom Style 123

Redefining an HTML tag 123

Using the CSS Selector 124

Editing styles 125

Creating an External Style Sheet 125

Adding styles 126

Linking a page to an External Style Sheet 126

Some useful references 126

9 Advanced formatting using layers and timelines . . . 129

Creating a layer 130

Putting content in a layer 132

Selecting a layer 132

Deleting a layer 132

Understanding layer properties 132

Working with layers 135

   Moving layers 135

   Positioning and aligning layers 135

   Nesting layers 136

   Overlapping layers 137

   Changing the stacking order of layers 138

   Changing layer visibility 138

Changing layer preferences 138

Converting layers to tables 140

Animating layers with a timeline 140

Getting to know the timeline 140

Creating animation along a timeline 142

Dragging an animation path 143

Editing layers in the timeline 144

Modifying timelines 144

Adding behaviours to a timeline 145

   Behaviour example 146

10 Working with behaviours 147

Attaching a behaviour to an object 148

Editing a behaviour 151

   Attaching an additional action 151

Changing the order of actions to be called 152

Changing the event associated with an action 152

Deleting a behaviour 152

Some common behaviours 153

Adding behaviours to Dreamweaver 155

11 **Templates, libraries and other assets** 157

Creating templates 158

Creating editable regions in a template 161

Creating new pages from a template 162

Attaching existing pages to a template 162

Detaching pages from a template 163

Changing template preferences 163

Creating library items 164

Inserting a library item 164

Editing a library item 165

Detaching objects from a library 166

Using the Assets panel 166

Using Assets from the site list 167

Adding assets to the Favorites list 168

Removing assets from the Favorites list 168

Creating a Favorites folder 168

12 Getting dynamic with databases 169

What you need to get started 171
Setting up Dreamweaver MX 173
Setting up a Testing Server 173
Setting up the database 173
Creating a DSN 175
Connecting to your database 176
Entering data fields in a page 179
Updating your database 184
Adding a record 184
Deleting a record 186
    Setting up the results page 186
    Working with the delete page 189
Some useful references 190

13 Managing and publishing your site 191

Running a spellcheck 192
Testing the site 192
Last-minute cleaning-up 194
Inserting keywords and a description 195
    How to use keywords 195
    Creating a description 197

Getting your site online 198
Setting up a remote site 198
Connecting to a remote server 200
Setting FTP preferences 201
Managing your site with Check In/Out 203
Using Design Notes 205

Appendices 209

Appendix A: Naming files 210
Appendix B: The Web-safe Color Palette 210
Appendix C: Setting up and testing a Web server 211
   To install a Web server 211
   To test your server 212

Index 213

Introduction

Dreamweaver MX is part of the MX Web development 'family' at Macromedia and offers a sophisticated development interface for both beginners and advanced users. Dreamweaver enables you to get your hands dirty with visible and accessible HTML code or lets you work in blissful ignorance while it builds code for you behind the scenes.

With Dreamweaver you can build a Website from scratch, integrate complex Web technologies and scripts on your page, develop dynamic Websites with database integration, test the site in different browsers, upload and download your site and manage your site in a team environment – all from within the program interface.

This guide is designed to help you get started in Dreamweaver and covers all of the major aspects of the program without getting bogged down in overly complex detail. Along the way you'll discover many tips and extras which should help you to use the program well, and also avoid many of the common pitfalls of building a Website.

System requirements

To install and run Dreamweaver MX you will need a computer with the following minimum hardware capacity.

For a PC running Microsoft Windows

- An Intel Pentium II processor or equivalent 300+ MHz running Windows 98, 2000, NT, ME or XP.
- Microsoft Internet Explorer or Netscape Navigator – in both cases Version 4 or later.
- 96 MB of available RAM (128 MB recommended by Macromedia).
- 275 MB available disk space.

For a Macintosh

- Power Mac G3 or better.
- Mac OS 9.1 or higher, or Mac OS X 10.1 or higher.
- Microsoft Internet Explorer or Netscape Navigator – in both cases Version 4 or later.
- 96 MB of available RAM (128 MB recommended by Macromedia).
- 275 MB available disk space.

Installing Dreamweaver

Installing software on your computer is very straightforward these days – and once you have started up the CD-ROM, the instructions should be clear and simple. To install Dreamweaver:

1. Insert the **CD-ROM**.

   In Windows go to **Start > Run**. Click **Browse** and choose the **Dreamweaver MX Installer.exe** file. Choose **OK** to begin the installation.

   On the Mac, find the **Dreamweaver Installer** icon and double-click to begin the installation.

2. Follow all of the on-screen instructions.

Keyboard and shortcut conventions

The *Simple Guide to Dreamweaver MX* is written for both PC and Mac users. Although the screenshots are all PC versions (sorry Mac users!), throughout the manual any shortcuts that differ between the systems will be written with the PC version first followed by the Mac version.

For example, the most common difference between the platforms is that with most PCs you have a two-button mouse allowing you to right-click to call up Context menus, and with a Mac you access the menus by holding down the Control key and clicking on the mouse. In this *Guide* both commands will be represented by '**Right/Ctrl-click**'.

In other circumstances, for instance where the instruction is Control + N on the PC and Command + N on the Mac, the shortcut will be written as **Ctrl/Cmd + N**.

Panel shortcuts

In Dreamweaver you can use the F-keys to open and close panels rather than having to always go to the Window drop-down menu. Because you use panels so frequently, you may find it really speeds up your work to get to know the commonly used panel shortcuts.

Panel	Windows	Macintosh
Insert Bar	Ctrl F2	Cmd F2
Property inspector	Ctrl F3	Cmd F3
Site Files	F8	F8
Databases	Shift Ctrl F10	Shift Cmd F10
Assets	F11	F11
Behaviors	Shift F3	Shift F3
CSS Styles	Shift F11	Shift F11
Frames	Shift F2	Shift F2
Layers	F2	F2

Adopted conventions

Throughout this book I have included notes, each of which is associated with an icon:

 Provides additional information about the subject covered.

 Provides suggestions and tips, including keyboard shortcuts, 'wizard' options, advanced techniques, etc.

} *Warns you of the risks associated with a particular action and, where necessary, shows you how to avoid any problems.*

*To quickly close all open panels use **F4**. To reopen as they were, hit **F4** again.*

What's in a Website?

What is HTML?

How does a Website get on to the Internet?

Planning a Website

Understanding the site goals

Identifying the site audience

Thinking about site navigation

What text?

Which images?

But is it dynamic?

Managing the Website

Some useful references

In this guide the term 'browser' refers to either Microsoft Internet Explorer or Netscape Navigator as they are the two most popular browsers available. Neither is given a preference, though it should be stressed that when you are developing a Website your pages should be checked on both browsers and on both platforms (PC and Mac) as pages may (and will) appear differently between them. For the latest statistics on who is using what browser it's worth visiting: www.BrowserWatch.com/stats.html.

While you may be a veteran user of the Internet and comfortably surf your way around Websites, send emails and so on, when it comes to building a site, one of the first questions people ask is, 'Well, what actually is a Website?' Well, these days a Website can be many things and can be made up of different elements and technologies. But to keep things simple, let's look at the basics. A Website is a collection of pages, or HTML files, that can display images, animations, movies and other media, and can draw content from a database. A Website is viewed in a Web browser and is accessed via the Internet. To get around a site, that is to go from page to page, the user follows hyperlinks, represented by underlined text or navigation 'buttons'.

What is HTML?

Most Web pages are written in a language called HyperText Markup Language or HTML. The HTML in a page consists of instructions, in HTML specifically known as 'tags', that tell the browser how to display page contents such as text and graphics.

Tags work by surrounding text with an opening <tag> and closing </tag> that tell the browser how the text should be displayed. In other instances a tag may instruct the browser to display a graphic or to link text to another page.

For example, to make a word bold you would surround it with the opening and closing bold tag, which looks like this: <B>. Therefore a line of text that displays in a browser like this:

Dreamweaver makes creating Web pages easy

would be created with the HTML code:

<B>Dreamweaver</B> makes creating Web pages easy.

Seem pretty straightforward? It is! And even if you are working with Dreamweaver (which is writing all that code for you) you will find that you will be a much more confident and capable Web developer if you have a working knowledge of HTML. For a start you can always dip into the code to troubleshoot problems on your page that Dreamweaver can't seem to sort (yes it does happen). You can also look at other people's code to see how they have put together particularly interesting things on their page.

If you are interested in learning HTML or want to expand on your existing knowledge you can work in Dreamweaver with the HTML code visible.

How does a Website get on to the Internet?

So how do you create a Website and make it available on the Internet? For most people who are novice Web developers this is the most mysterious part – when and how does the site get 'live'? The outline below and the accompanying diagram (Figure 1.1) may help to explain.

1. You create the Website *locally*, that is on your hard drive or local network.
2. Once the site has been tested and is ready to go live you 'upload' the files to a host server. To do this you need to have various things in place:
   (a) A **Host Server** – which is where your site is going to be accessed via the Internet.
   (b) A **modem** to connect to the server.
   (c) A Web address, or **Domain Name** (also known as a **URL**: Uniform Resource Locator), so Internet users can access your site.

For more on working in the code view see the section in Chapter 2: The Document window (see Chapter 2: The Dreamweaver MX workspace).

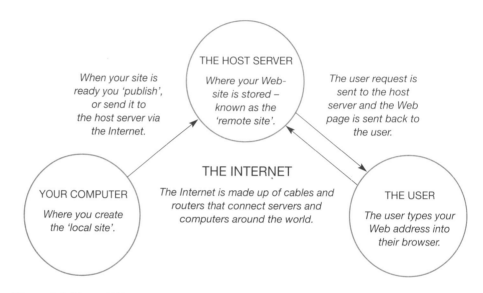

Figure 1.1 How a Website goes live.

3. To upload your files to the server you need to use a process called **FTP**: File Transfer Protocol. Dreamweaver comes with FTP installed and makes the process of uploading fairly straightforward and stress free.

4. Your site is now 'live' on the Internet!

5. When you need to make changes or updates to the site you do so on the local site and then upload the pages again to the server and the 'live' files will be overwritten.

Planning a Website

A site that has a well-thought out structure and is clear in both purpose and presentation will be appreciated by visitors and should encourage them to return. Whether information is easy to find on a site and whether the user finds the experience satisfying will ultimately come down to good, solid planning.

The question of planning a Website is not simply one of content and design in the traditional sense. If you have created a brochure for print, the final, printed version is what everyone sees. In the big, bad world of the Web you can never be so sure of the end result. Is the user seeing the site on an old Mac or are they using a jazzy new PC laptop? You just don't know. But the more time you spend defining the possibilities and testing for different user scenarios, the more manageable the great unknown becomes.

So, the first stage of building a Website is the planning process. You may find it useful to consider some of the issues raised below and, where relevant, discuss them with other members of the team and with your clients. What you want to avoid are issues being raised well into the production stage which should have been addressed from the word go.

Understanding the site goals

The planning stage of a Website can't really get started until you determine what the site is about and what are its goals. If you are developing your own site, try listing what you hope the site will achieve, with whom and in what time frame.

If you are developing the site for a client (and the 'client' can often be represented by more than one person) this process is all the more important. You need to establish that the client is clear about what they want the site to achieve and be sure that you understand those goals and are in full agreement.

Often when you go through the process of agreeing on goals, problems can be avoided and inevitably time and money saved!

Identifying the site audience

Knowing your target audience is important in Website development, not only for the obvious purpose of content and message delivery but also for the more technical consideration of site functionality. Pages appear and perform differently depending upon the users' systems, or platforms, browsers, screens and modem speed.

Ask some simple questions and keep them in mind when designing, building and testing your site:

- What platform are they using – PC or Mac?
- What screen resolution do they use and how many colours can their screen display?
- What modem speed will they be connecting via?
- Will they be viewing the page from behind some sort of Internet security system, such as a corporate firewall, which may limit the types of pages they can view?
- What browser will they be using, Microsoft's Internet Explorer or Netscape's Navigator, and which version?

You'll probably find the answer to some of these questions is something like: 'possibly all', 'maybe/maybe not' or 'how would I know?' That's what designing for the Web is all about! The most you can do is to develop a user profile with the information you have available, tailor your site to that profile and TEST, TEST, TEST. It is not mandatory that every site works in every possible set-up, but your responsibility as the Web developer lies in knowing *where* it doesn't work and *why*.

Thinking about site navigation

Put yourself in the shoes of the user. Is it easy to navigate around the site? Can you move between pages quickly and intuitively? If you return to the site will you be able to get to a particular page quickly? (Waiting for that intro-animation sequence to finish for the third time can be really annoying …)

One of the main reasons why visitors leave sites prematurely, or choose not to buy products, is an over-complicated user interface and confusing navigation. So keep it clear and simple. Try testing your navigation on users with no knowledge of the site: watch and note how they approach the site and if it's applicable, set them a task to find a certain bit of information and see how long (and how many mistakes) it takes them to get there.

What text?

Planning and organising the content of the site is important for several reasons. The first, and most obvious, is that the copy for your page must be just as rigorously planned and well-written as any published material. Always spellcheck pages and if possible proofread text from a printed page. You might consider employing a copywriter who specialises in Web text, as reading copy on-screen has different implications for the user from reading print.

As far as possible try to avoid excessively long pages of text. You might find it useful to look at information sites (such as newspaper or government Websites) to see how they handle large text documents and whether you, as a user, find

For more on creating PDF files visit the Adobe Acrobat Website at www.adobe.com.

the information accessible. If you absolutely must deliver a lot of text in one block you could always consider displaying a short extract and create a **PDF** (Portable Document Format) version that users can download and print from.

Another consideration when writing text for your site is whether you want to target **Search Engines**. Many search engines consider the text in your page, particularly the text closest to the top of the page, as important when indexing your site for keywords. Think about which search terms and keywords people might use when searching for a site like yours and try to include them in your page. For more on optimising your site for search engines see the section in Chapter 13: Inserting keywords and a description.

Which images?

Images are an essential part of most Websites but there are still some issues to consider on how best to incorporate graphics in a site. Do they enhance your site and do they complement the site content? Are they worth the wait? Are they really necessary? Graphics generally do enhance a Web page and are, in many cases, essential. You just have to keep in mind the extra download time that graphics create and be considerate to your user.

If you really must display large graphics consider displaying a thumbnail (or small version) and giving the user the choice to click to another page to view the full, or large, version. It is also useful to let them know the size (in bytes) of the larger graphic so they can estimate how long it will take to download.

But is it dynamic?

A 'dynamic' Website is really what it's all about these days and that's not to say that you just add some groovy colours to your page and wait for someone to say 'Wow, your site looks great…it's so DYNAMIC!' It actually refers to the way your site works.

A traditional HTML page that is called up and sits unchanging in the Web browser is known as a 'static' page. The user has no input and the page is always the same no matter when or where it is requested. Dynamic pages are a tad more sophisticated.

In one sense a dynamic page can be defined as one that is built using Dynamic HTML (DHTML). DHTML can combine all sorts of technologies, such as JavaScript, to create interactive elements on a page, such as mouse rollovers.

Another use of the term, and the way it is mainly used with Dreamweaver MX, is that a site is database driven. If you have content that changes frequently, or if you want to collect information or orders from your site, you may want to consider developing a database to run with your site. For more on database integration, see Chapter 12: Getting dynamic with databases.

Managing the Website

Site planning is not just about the user experience, that is the content and navigation of the site, it is also about file management. As soon as you start building even a small site you'll find yourself with a multitude of graphics and HTML files.

*Keep in mind that some users accessing your site may not be able to view graphics at all. Voice browsers read the text in a Web page so think about how your site will 'read' and the implications this may have on your design. With this in mind you should always add **Alt text** to images (for an explanation of the Alt tag and how to use it refer to the section in Chapter 4: Image properties). Other people surf the Web with the images option turned off in their browser preferences. It makes it faster for them to get around!*

A simple way to manage a small site is to divide your files into folders according to type: HTML files in one folder, images in another, Flash animations in another and so on. For an example of a simple file management structure see Figure 1.2.

For larger, more complex sites you may decide to subdivide whole sections of files into separate folders, such as Clients or Products, and keep your HTML and other sub-folders within them. In many cases the way that site files and folders are organised will directly reflect the way the sections of the Website are divided, for instance sections for Clients, Products, Contact details.

Time spent planning how to manage your files will pay off in the long run. Not only will it be easier for you to locate files, but it will make collaborative site work simpler and make a future transition smoother for someone taking over a site. It's a simple karmic principle: what goes around comes around!

Some useful references

If you are working as part of a large Web team you may want to further explore the development and planning process. An excellent book on that topic is: Jessica Burdman, *Collaborative Web Development: Strategies and Best Practices for Web Teams*, Addison-Wesley, 1999.

To find out more about usability testing a useful place to start is with the usability guru Jacob Nielsen. Visit his site at www.useit.com

An excellent reference for learning more about structuring a site is: Louis Rosenfeld and Peter Morville, *Information Architecture for the World Wide Web*, O'Reilly, 1998.

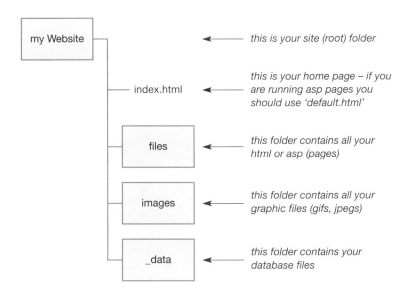

this is your site (root) folder

this is your home page – if you
are running asp pages you
should use 'default.html'

this folder contains all your
html or asp (pages)

this folder contains all your
graphic files (gifs, jpegs)

this folder contains your
database files

Figure 1.2 File management structure.

*In the diagram you will notice
that the home page is called
index.html. This is a default
name that all browsers will
recognise as the first page to
open in a Website – therefore the home or welcome
page. For a further explanation, refer to Appendix A:
Naming files.*

Getting started in Dreamweaver

2

The Dreamweaver MX workspace

Setting up a site in Dreamweaver

Working with files and folders

Opening an existing site in Dreamweaver

Deleting a site from the Site window

Changing the look of the Site window

Using the Site Map

Printing the Site Map

This chapter introduces you to the Dreamweaver MX environment. If you are totally new to creating Websites many of the menus and their functions won't mean that much at this stage, but don't worry, the purpose of the first half of this chapter is not to confuse you but simply to familiarise you with the Dreamweaver layout. The more panels and menus you access, the more quickly you'll be able to find your way around the program and confidently use different features.

The Dreamweaver MX workspace

When you start up Dreamweaver MX for the first time Windows users are given the option of choosing between two different Dreamweaver MX environments. One is a fixed window layout and the other is a floating layout. Both layouts offer the same development options but simply differ in the way they are positioned on the page. For Mac users only the floating option is available.

The fixed window layout (Figure 2.1) is probably the easiest to work with as you don't need to be constantly moving panels around the screen to see what's hidden underneath.

*You can change the workspace at any time by going to **Edit > Preferences > General > Change Workspace** and selecting the workspace you want to change to.*

The floating panel layout (Figure 2.2) will be familiar to those used to working with Dreamweaver 4 and is the only option available to Mac users. All of the panels and windows are floating as individual elements on the screen, though you will find that they do 'snap' together when you move them close which helps to keep them organised.

The Document window

In Dreamweaver you have the choice of working in three different 'views' in the Document window (Figure 2.3). One is known as Design view and is very similar to working in a word processing package – you type and edit directly into the document window – absolutely no code in sight!

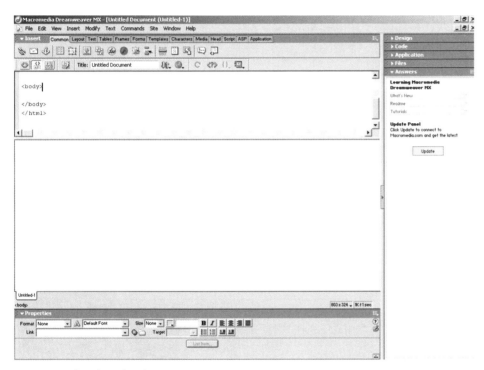

Figure 2.1 Fixed window layout.

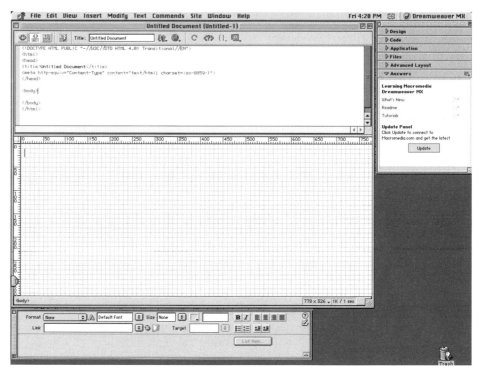

Figure 2.2 Floating panel layout (on a Mac).

Figure 2.3 Different Document window views.

Another option is to work with a split screen, known as Code and Design view, enabling you to work in Design view in the lower half and view the HTML code in the top half.

The final option is the Code view, which displays only the HTML code.

You can choose between the view options by using the buttons displayed in the Toolbar, which is described in the next section. You may also notice on the Toolbar that you have an option called Live Data View. This is for when you are inserting content from a database and it allows you to see how the page will actually appear in the browser window. For more on working with Live Data View, see Chapter 12: Getting dynamic with databases.

The Toolbar

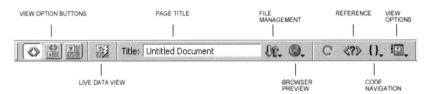

Figure 2.4 The Toolbar.

*To turn the Toolbar on/off go to **View > Toolbar**.*

You can access many of the most commonly used commands in Dreamweaver using the **Toolbar** (Figure 2.4). It is here that you can toggle between the different document view options. You can also set your page title, which is explained in the section in Chapter 3: Setting the Page Properties, preview your files in a browser and set view options for the different views.

The Status bar

Figure 2.5 The Status bar.

Along the bottom of the Document window is the Status bar which displays, from left:

1. The Tag selector, which displays current HTML tags and allows you to easily select a current tag.

2. The Window size drop-down menu. The page sizes displayed here give you an indication of the ideal page size for different monitor resolutions. For example, for a resolution of 800×600 the page size should be 760×420 to allow for space taken up by the browser and by the operating system on Windows and on the Mac. It is important to realise that Dreamweaver is not really setting a page size here but simply allowing you to see how your page will view at that particular screen resolution. You actually set the page size using either tables or layers, which are both covered in detail in later chapters.

3. The Page size 'weight' of the page in bytes, which also estimates how long the page will take to download for a visitor using a 28.8 kbps modem.

4. The Launcher Bar is a shortcut for opening commonly used panels. If the Launcher Bar is not appearing, go to **Edit > Preferences > Panels** and click the **Show Icons** tab in the **Panels and Launcher** box.

*You can set your own Status bar preferences for different window sizes, download times and to turn the Launcher Bar on/off. To make changes go to **Edit > Preferences > Status bar**. You can also add or delete items from the Launcher Bar by going to **Edit > Preferences > Panels**.*

The Property inspector

It is in the Property inspector that you will do most of your text, layout and image editing (Figure 2.6). Depending on which object you have selected, the inspector displays all of the editing options available for that object. Note the small arrow at the bottom right of the inspector which expands and collapses the window. It's generally a good idea to leave the inspector fully expanded so that you don't miss out on any formatting options.

Figure 2.6 The Property inspector.

*All of the panels in Dreamweaver can be opened and closed from the **Window** drop-down menu in the Dreamweaver Main window. You may find it useful to memorise the F-key shortcuts for the panels you use most frequently. See the Introduction for a list of useful F-key shortcuts.*

The Insert bar

The **Insert** bar is where you insert objects, such as images, Flash movies or record sets from a database, onto your pages. From the **Insert** bar you can also select frame layouts or decide which table mode to work in. As you can see in Figure 2.7, the different insert categories are displayed in tabs along the top of the bar and when you select a tab the relevant options appear below.

The categories are:

- **Common**: contains commonly used objects such as images, layers and Flash movies.
- **Layout**: selects how you want to work – with tables in standard or layout mode, or with layers.

Figure 2.7 The Insert bar.

- **Text**: options for formatting text on the page.
- **Tables**: enables you to insert tables and, if you are familiar with HTML, insert particular table tags.
- **Frames**: provides some pre-formatted framesets.
- **Forms**: contains all the elements needed to create response forms.
- **Templates**: contains options for saving a page as a site template and inserting template regions.
- **Characters**: lists special characters such as accented letters and symbols such as copyright.
- **Media**: provides options for inserting other media such as Flash movies or Java applets.
- **Head**: used for adding background information to your page. The information sits in the <HEAD> tag of the page and is commonly contained in a <META> tag. For example a META tag may contain a description of your site that will be picked up by search engines.
- **Script**: enables you to add scripts to your page.
- **ASP**: depending on the server language selected for a page, the tab will contain options for inserting code and objects available for that language.
- **Application**: used to add database-related elements to your page.

*Many of the options available in the **Insert** bar can also be found in the Insert drop-down menu along the top of the screen.*

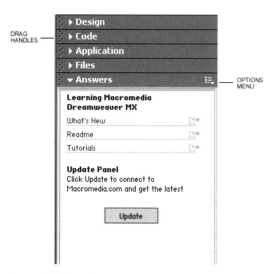

Figure 2.8 Panel groups.

Panel groups

In Dreamweaver MX editing and formatting options are displayed in panels. In previous versions of Dreamweaver one of the common complaints was that the window was very messy with lots of panels floating around. By grouping panels together, as you can see in Figure 2.8, the workspace doesn't look too chaotic...well not yet anyway!

One of the great features of using Dreamweaver is that the workspace is cus-tomisable, for instance you can change the name of a panel group by clicking on the options menu found on the right of the Panel group title bar (making sure that the panel is open first). You can also dock or undock panels by click-ing and dragging the handle found on the left of the Panel group title bar.

- **Design**: contains the CSS, HTML Styles and Behaviors panels.
- **Code**: access to the Tag Inspector, Snippets and Reference.
- **Application**: access to Databases, Bindings, Server Behaviors and Components.
- **Files**: displays the Assets manager.
- **Advanced Layout**: contains panels for working with layers and frames.
- **History**: records all the previous steps within the current document. From within the panel you can move the slider bar up to go back multiple steps.
- **Answers**: provides access to tutorials and news about Dreamweaver MX.

Other panels are available for inserting and modifying other Dreamweaver functions such as timelines. These panels are accessed from the Window drop-down menu. You may want to get to know the shortcuts for opening and closing panels, listed in the Introduction.

Using Context menus
Context menus display commands relating to a selected object, or to the window in which you are working. To access the menus, make your selection then **Right/Ctrl-click** (Figure 2.9).

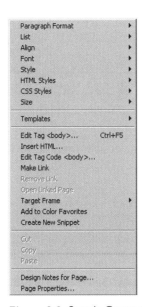

Figure 2.9 Sample Context menu.

Setting up a site in Dreamweaver

'Setting up a site' probably sounds fairly boring when all you are dying to do is get going and start creating pages – but it's actually really important that you do it *before* starting work in Dreamweaver. By setting up a site in Dreamweaver you are simply telling the program where your site is going to be kept on your hard drive so that automated program functions (such as linking pages) can be applied properly – pretty powerful stuff really.

To enable you to set up a site it is important that you create a folder on your system for all your site files. This folder is referred to in Dreamweaver as your local site. As mentioned in Chapter 1: Managing the Website you should think about how you are going to organise your site files. One simple system is to separate your HTML files and image files into different sub-folders within your site folder. Have a look at the site structure set out in Figure 1.2, which you may find helpful to get you started.

Your site folder should contain only those files that are going to be part of the final published site – those files which will be uploaded to the Web server. Any other files, such as word documents, scanned photographs and so on, should be kept separately – perhaps in a folder called 'Working documents' or anything that clearly distinguishes them from your site files.

To get started in Dreamweaver we are going to set up a local site. In later chapters we will go through how to get the site 'live' by setting up a remote site, and also how to work with a database and set up a testing server.

To set up a site in Dreamweaver:

1. In the main Dreamweaver window, go to **Site > New Site**.
2. In the **Site Definition** window you are now presented with the site set-up wizard, which appears if the Basic tab is selected at the top of the window and is recommended if you are new to the program. If you have already worked with previous versions of Dreamweaver you may prefer to select the **Advanced** tab and set up as you have before (see Figure 2.10).
3. Enter a name for your site. The name you enter here is for your reference only and won't be published online. Click on the **Next** button.

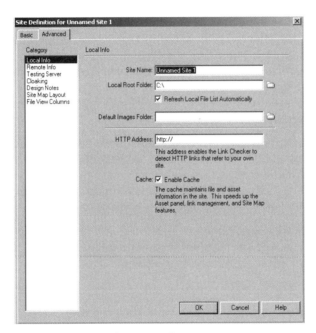

Figure 2.10 Site Definition window.

4. Select the **No I do not want to use a sever technology** button and then click on the **Next** button.

5. Select the **Edit local copies** button and then use the folder icon and navigate to and select the folder you have set up to contain your files. Click on the **Next** button.

6. Choose **I'll set this up later** from the drop-down menu and click on the **Next** button.

7. Check the summary and click on the **Done** button.

8. The initial cache will now be created which is a local memory and which speeds up Dreamweaver functions such as creating links. You should also be aware that the site Assets panel will work only if a site cache has been created.

9. Your site will now appear in the Local Site area of the Site panel found under the Files panel group. Expand the window to view your files more easily by using the **Expand/Collapse** button on the right of the panel (Figure 2.11). Not much there yet...but you are now ready to go and create pages!

*Important! Step 5 varies slightly between the PC and Mac platforms. If you are working on a PC you actually open the folder and then choose **Select**, but if you are working on a Mac you simply highlight the folder name (do not double-click to go into the folder) and choose **Select**.*

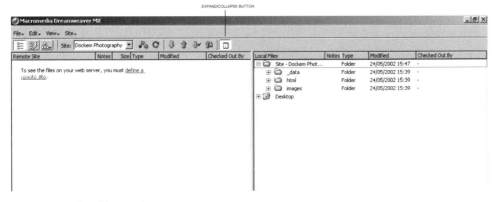

Figure 2.11 Site Files window.

*Use the **expand/collapse** button to view larger file definition.*

For information and tips on file names and conventions see Appendix A: Naming files.

Working with files and folders

You can create and delete files and folders from within the Site Files window. You can also move files and folders within the window and Dreamweaver will update any links to and from those files – guaranteed to be one of the most useful features in the Dreamweaver Site Files window!

To create a new file from within the Site Files window:

1. Go to **File > New File** (**Ctrl + Shift + N**) (PC).

   Or

   Go to **Site > Site Files View > New File** (**Cmd + Shift + N**) (Mac).

2. Enter a name for your new file.

3. Double-click on the file icon in the **Site** window to open the file.

To create a new folder:

1. Go to **File > New Folder** (**Ctrl + Alt + Shift + N**) (PC).

   Or

   Go to **Site > Site Files View > New Folder** (**Cmd + Alt + Shift + N**) (Mac).

2. Enter the name of the new folder.

To delete files and folders:

1. In the **Site** window highlight the file or folder and press the **Delete** or **Backspace** key.

2. A dialog box will appear to confirm the command, so click **OK**.

Opening an existing site in Dreamweaver

A site does not have to have been created in Dreamweaver for you to be able to work with it and edit it in the program. As long as the pages are written in HTML they should appear in Dreamweaver as normal.

To add an existing site to your Site window, follow the same instructions as for **Setting up a site in Dreamweaver** and select the existing site folder.

Deleting a site from the Site window

1. Go to **Site > Edit Sites**.
2. Highlight the site you want to delete and click the **Remove** button.

Dreamweaver will delete the site from the Site window but (don't worry!) it will not delete the site from your local or remote system.

Changing the look of the Site window

There are various changes you can make to the Site window view.

- If you are only working locally and do not wish to view the Remote Site files area you can collapse the window by clicking on the small arrow on the bottom left-hand side of the Site window.

- You can also increase or decrease the width of the site columns such as Local Folder and Size Type by dragging the bar that separates the column names.

Be aware that if you delete a folder in the Site window, all the files in that folder will automatically be deleted.

Using the Site Map

The Site Map will only view if you have identified a home page, from which Dreamweaver can create a site structure. If you are not using a default home page name such as 'index.html' then you should identify a welcome or home page by going to **Site > Edit Sites > Choose a Site and click Edit > Site Map Layout**. To learn more about naming files and setting up a home page see Appendix A: Naming files.

To view the structure of your site click on the **Site Map** button on the top centre of the Site window.

*In the **Site Map** look out for broken links indicated in red!*

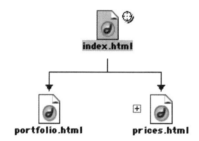

Figure 2.12 The Site Map.

Dreamweaver displays linked files in the order in which the links appear in each page. By default, the site structure will display the first two levels starting from the home page (Figure 2.12). Any deeper than that and a plus (+) sign will appear beside the page icon which you can click to view linked files.

Links to other sites or email links will be displayed next to a Globe symbol.

Printing the Site Map

There is no easy command to print the Site Map from Dreamweaver – which is a shame as it can be a useful tool for discussing the site structure with clients and/or colleagues. To create a printable version of the Site Map you have to save it as an image file and then print it from either a browser or an image-editing program.

The options you get vary between the PC and Mac platforms.

- If you are working on a PC go to **File > Save Site Map** and enter a name and file type (either **.bmp** or **.png**). Choose where to save the file and click **OK**.

- If you are working on a Mac go to **Site > Site Map View > Save Site Map** and select whether you want to save as a PICT or a JPEG. Name the file and choose where you want to save it and click **Save**.

Creating a basic Web page

3

Opening a page

Setting the Page Properties

Creating and formatting text

Paragraphs and line breaks

Inserting and editing horizontal rules

Using special characters

Working with lists

Importing text created in Microsoft Word

Saving a page

Previewing the page in a browser

Printing a page

OK ... it's finally time to start building some Web pages!

In this chapter we are going to go through the basic page editing options to get you started: opening and saving pages, setting background and default text colours and formatting text and paragraphs, and also seeing how the page looks in a Web browser.

It is important to realise that the text formatting options outlined in this chapter are straightforward HTML options that will be visible across browsers and most importantly are simple to apply! When you get the hang of creating pages and further developing your site you may prefer to start using CSS styles, which are explained in Chapter 8 and offer a much greater range of formatting options. Using CSS is how all Web pages will be formatted in the future so they are worth getting used to.

Opening a page

To get started let's open a new page.

1. Go to **File > New (Ctrl/Cmd + N)**.
2. In the New Window dialog box (Figure 3.1) make sure the General tab is selected and choose Basic Page and highlight HTML.
3. Click the Create button.

To open an existing page:

1. Go to **File > Open** (**Ctrl/Cmd + O**).
2. Navigate to your file and click the **Open** button.

If you want to add pages to your site that were created elsewhere, for example documents created in Microsoft Word then saved as HTML, you need to add them to your site folder so that they can be recognised within the Dreamweaver site environment. For more on importing Microsoft Word documents, see the section Importing text created in Microsoft Word later in this chapter.

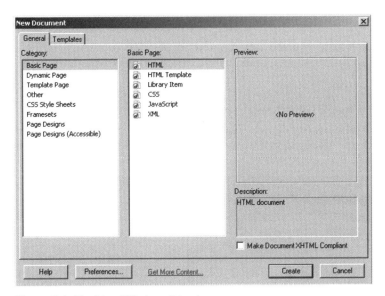

Figure 3.1 The New Window dialog box.

You can open any HTML page in Dreamweaver including those that have been created in previous versions of Dreamweaver, in other HTML editing packages or those hand-coded in a basic text-editing program such as Notepad.

You can also open pages by opening the Site window (F8) and double-clicking on the file icon. (If you double-click on the file *name*, Dreamweaver will interpret your command as a wish to change the file name, so make sure you click directly on the file **icon**.)

Setting the Page Properties

Page Properties are where you set your page title, select colours for the page background, text and links, select a background image and set page margins.

To access Page Properties:

1. Go to **Modify > Page Properties** (**Ctrl/Cmd + J**).
2. In the **Page Properties** dialog box (Figure 3.2) make your selections, then click **OK** (or click on **Apply** if you want to view the changes before deciding on a selection).

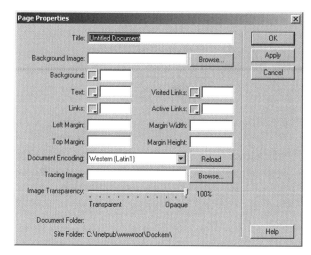

Figure 3.2 The Page Properties.

The most important properties for you to start with are:

- **Page title**. The page title does not appear in your Web page at all, but actually appears at the top of the browser window (Figure 3.3). It is easy to confuse the page title with the file name, but remember that they are completely different. The file name is what you call the file when you first save it and it will always end with an extension .htm. The 'title' of a Web page is also used by Web browsers to identify a page in a 'Bookmarks' or 'Favorites' list. Some search engines also rank page titles as significant when indexing site pages for keywords.

You can also set the page title from the Main window Toolbar.

Figure 3.3 The page title appearing in the browser.

Background images can also be used on a table (more on tables in Chapter 5) and when using style sheets, where you can control how and if the image repeats and where it should be positioned on a page (see Chapter 8: Advanced formatting using styles).

- **Background image**. Use the **Browse** button to select a background image that will be automatically tiled, or repeated, to fit the browser window.
- **Background**. Click on the **Color picker** box and use the **Eyedropper** tool to select a background colour for your page. When you create a new page in Dreamweaver the default background colour is set to white (#FFFFFF).
- **Text**. Click on the **Color picker** box and use the **Eyedropper** tool to select a text colour for the page.
- **Links**. Set a link colour for the page.

For more on using colour on the Web see Appendix B: The Web-safe Color Palette.

■ **Visited Links**. Set a visited link colour for the page. You may have noticed when using the Internet that if you follow a link to a Website, when you return to the page with that link it will have changed colour. Yes? Well, that is the 'visited link' colour that you're seeing.

■ **Active Links**. Set an active link colour for the page. An active link colour appears when the user clicks on the link – usually only a flash before the new page is called up. If the user follows a link and then uses that **Back** button to return to the page with the link, the active link colour may still be visible in some browsers.

Creating and formatting text

The easiest way to create text in Dreamweaver is to type directly into the document window. Once you've got some text on the page you use the Property inspector to apply formatting options and select font type, colour, size and style.

■ **To format a selection of text**. Highlight the text in the **document window** and make your changes in the **Property inspector** (Figure 3.4).

■ **To create a heading**. Choose from the **Heading** options in the **Format** drop-down menu. Heading 1 is the largest size and Heading 6 is the smallest. When you apply a Heading size to text you will also see that the text appears in bold and will be followed by a paragraph break.

■ **To select a font**. Select a font face from the drop-down menu in the **Property inspector**.

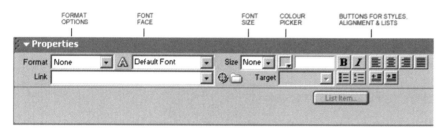

Figure 3.4 Text formatting options.

When you specify a font in a Web page the browser can only display that font if it is installed on the user's system. Therefore, you will notice in Dreamweaver that there is more than one font in a single selection, for example: **Verdana**, **Arial**, **Helvetica**, **sans-serif** which gives the browser a selection of fonts to find on the system. The first font in the group, or font 'string', should be your preferred font, with other options following sequentially after that.

To add your own string of fonts to the drop-down menu:

1. From the **Font** drop-down menu in the Property inspector, select **Edit Font List** to access the Edit Font List window (Figure 3.5).

2. Go to **Available Fonts** and scroll to select a font.

3. Use the arrow button on the left of the Available Fonts window to add it to the **Chosen Fonts** window.

4. Continue adding fonts with the across arrow to create a font string.

5. Use the (+) button to add a new group of fonts.

Setting relative font sizes is a very 'user-friendly' way of working. Users with visual impairments may choose to set their browser default font size to, say a '4'. If you use relative sizes then you are working with their default size rather than trying to change it. For example, you could decide to leave your body copy at the user's default settings (not specifying a size at all) then set all of your headings as '+2', subheadings as '+1' and footers as '–1'.

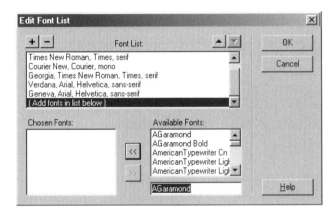

Figure 3.5 Edit Font List window.

■ **To change the size of text**. On most browsers the default size of text is a font size of 3. Use the **Size** drop-down menu in the **Property** inspector to select a font size between 1 and 7, size 1 being the smallest. Alternatively you can choose a relative size using the (+) or (–) options. If you set a relative size, the font displayed will be directly related to the default size specified in the user's browser. For example, if the user's browser is set at the default setting of '3', and you specify in the page a font size of '–1' then the text will be displayed in the browser as a size '2'.

■ **To change the text colour**. Click on the colour box to access the Color picker and select a text colour.

■ **To apply bold and italic styles**. Use the bold and italic buttons in the **Property inspector** – they should look pretty familiar (Figure 3.4)!

Paragraphs and line breaks

When you type text into the document window and press the **Return** (Enter) key, Dreamweaver will insert a paragraph break around your text (in the HTML code there will be a <P> tag surrounding your text). Why this is significant is that it plays a part in how you can align paragraphs, or blocks of text, and how you can apply styles to blocks of text (coming later in Chapter 8: Advanced formatting using styles).

Aligning paragraphs

You will find that text layout options are fairly basic at this stage: left, centre and right! To align blocks, or paragraphs, of text:

1. Highlight a block of text or place your cursor within a paragraph.

2. In the **Property inspector** select one of the alignment options (Figure 3.4).

Indenting paragraphs

1. Highlight a block of text or place your cursor within a paragraph.

2. In the **Property inspector** select the **Indent** button (Figure 3.4). Repeat-click to indent text again.

3. Use the **Outdent** button to reverse any indent formatting.

Inserting line breaks

If you don't want to insert a paragraph break between blocks of text (such as you would get if you hit the Return/Enter key) but just want to break to the next line, you need to insert a line break (represented by a <BR> tag in the HTML). For instance, if you wanted to write an address:

You may notice that Dreamweaver inserts the HTML code <STRONG> for bold and <EM> for italics. This provides instructions for a voice browser on how to read the text.

The HTML tag creating the indent is <BLOCKQUOTE>. When you add multiple indents, in the HTML you will see multiple <BLOCK-QUOTE> tags surrounding your text. There is no option to set the size of Indent or Outdent.

Mr I. Smith
10 Waterstone Crescent
London W2 NPY.

To insert a line break hold down the **Shift** key when you hit **Return/Enter**.

Inserting and editing horizontal rules

Horizontal rules are those familiar grey lines that are used on Web pages to separate blocks of text. The HTML tag for a horizontal rule is <HR>.

To insert a horizontal line:

1. Place your cursor where you want the line to be.

2. On the **Insert** bar select the **Insert Horizontal Rule** button, which is found on the **Common** tab.

   Or

   Go to **Insert > Horizontal Rule**.

A line will be inserted and the formatting options will appear in the Property inspector (Figure 3.6).

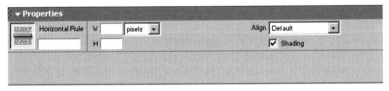

Figure 3.6 Horizontal Rule options.

The formatting options are:

- **Width**. You can assign a set width in pixels or a flexible width as a percentage of the browser window.
- **Height**. Set in pixels.
- **Shading**. Fills the line to a block colour, rather than a bevel.
- **Alignment**. Left, right or centre (the default is centre).

Using special characters

In HTML code there are certain characters that are not properly recognised by Web browsers if you type them in directly from the keyboard. Some examples are the pound (£) symbol, and characters with accents. Instead of using the keyboard shortcuts to insert these characters use the HTML 'Special Characters' which are available in Dreamweaver.

To insert a special character:

In the **Insert** bar select the **Characters** tab and choose from the available buttons (Figure 3.7).

To add characters with accents or to access more options select the **Others** button in the **Characters** option.

Or

1. Place the cursor where you want the character to appear.
2. Go to **Insert > Special Characters** and select from the list.

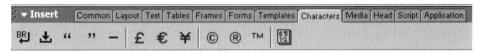

Figure 3.7 HTML Special Characters.

Working with lists

You can easily create numbered lists and bullet point lists in Dreamweaver, known in HTML as ordered lists <OL> and unordered lists <UL> respectively.

To create a numbered list:

1. Make a list of items separated by returns.
2. Select the list.
3. In the **Property inspector** select the **Ordered List** button (Figure 3.4).

To create a list with bullet points:

1. Follow points 1 and 2 above.
2. In the **Property inspector** select the **Unordered List** button (Figure 3.4).

To add new items to a list:

1. Place the cursor at the end of the line before the place where you want the new item to appear.
2. Click **Enter/Return** and type in the new item.

To delete an item from a list:

Highlight the item to delete and press **Delete/Backspace** twice (once to remove the item and again to remove the line).

You should also use the Special Characters list to insert character spaces on your page. You will notice that if you repeatedly press the space bar to create space, Dreamweaver won't recognise more than one. To insert a space choose the **Non-breaking Space** *button.*

Importing text created in Microsoft Word

You can copy and paste text created in Microsoft Word directly into Dreamweaver but you may lose important formatting elements in the process. Instead, you will have better results if you use the '**Save as HTML**' option in Microsoft Word and run a clean-up operation in Dreamweaver. The reason you need to 'clean up' Microsoft Word HTML files is that the code it produces is usually fairly bulky, with lots of extra, unnecessary tags.

*To add a line between your list items press **Shift Enter/Return** twice.*

There are two ways of properly converting Word documents in Dreamweaver:

1. (a) Save the document in Microsoft Word using the 'Save as HTML' option in the Word Edit menu.

   (b) In Dreamweaver choose **File > Import > Word HTML** and select the file saved as HTML.

   (c) Dreamweaver will open the file and automatically open the **Clean Up Word HTML** dialog box.

   (d) In the dialog box (Figure 3.8) leave the default settings to clean up all aspects of the document, or make the changes you prefer.

Or

2. (a) Save the document in Microsoft Word using the **Save as HTML** option in the **Edit** menu.

   (b) In Dreamweaver select **File > Open** and select the file saved as HTML.

   (c) Go to **Commands > Clean up Word HTML**.

   (d) Make your selections as above.

When you are saving your first, or 'home' page, save it as 'index.html', on the root level of your site. This sets the page as your default home page. For more on setting up your site files, see Chapter 1 and Figure 1.2, and for more on naming conventions refer to Appendix A: Naming files.

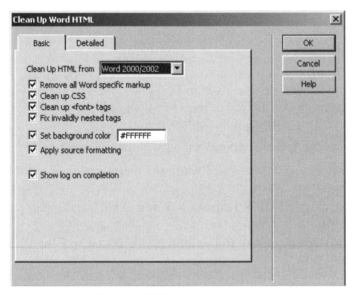

Figure 3.8 Clean Up Word HTML.

Saving a page

To save your page in Dreamweaver:

1. Go to **File > Save (Ctrl/Cmd + S)**.

2. Name the file (Dreamweaver will automatically insert the file extension) and make sure you save it in the appropriate site folder.

To save a copy of your page:

1. Go to **File > Save As**.

2. Type in a new name for your file and save it in the appropriate site folder.

Once your file is saved it will appear in the Site window, which you can quickly access at any time by pressing the F8 key.

Previewing the page in a browser

Although in the Dreamweaver document window you can see how your page *should* look on the Web, you can't really be sure that it will appear properly until you preview it in a Web browser. It's also only from within the browser that you can check the page functionality (such as links) and also check any differences between browser types and versions.

To preview your page:

From the Toolbar click on the **Globe** icon and select which browser you would like to preview in (your selection options will depend on what browsers you have installed on your system) (Figure 3.9).

*Always spellcheck! There is nothing worse than a page full of spelling errors. To run a spellcheck go to **Text > Check Spelling (Shift + F7)**. To change the dictionary, say from US to UK, go to **Edit > Preferences > General**, and select the dictionary from the drop-down menu.*

Figure 3.9 The Toolbar browser option.

Or

1. Go to **File > Preview in Browser**.

2. Select the browser name.

Familiarise yourself with the shortcuts for previewing in the browser – **F12** for your primary browser, which is the one you use most frequently, and **Ctrl/Cmd +F12** for your secondary browser – worth remembering as they're shortcuts you'll use all the time!

To add browsers to the Preview option:

1. Go to the Toolbar, click on the **Globe** icon and select **Edit Browser List** (you will find this actually opens up your **Preferences** window) (Figure 3.10).

2. From the **Preferences** window click on the browsers **plus (+)** button to add a browser.

3. Use the **Browse** button to locate a browser on your system.

4. Check a box to make it **Primary** or **Secondary**.

Printing a page

You can't print directly from the Dreamweaver window so you have to preview your page first in a browser and print from there.

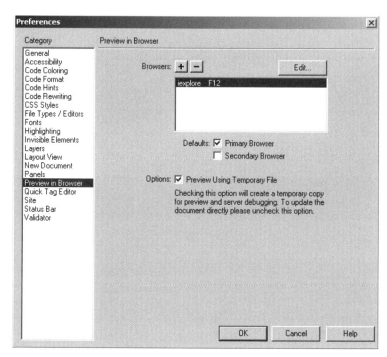

Figure 3.10 Browser preferences.

Images and links

4

Inserting an image

Image properties

Resizing an image

Image alignment

Creating links

Linking using jump menus

Linking with image maps

Creating a simple mouse rollover

So far you have a static page or two with text and colour. It's now time to start jazzing it up a bit by inserting some graphics and linking some pages – the essence of a real Website.

Inserting an image

When you insert an image on the page in Dreamweaver, the image is not **embedded**, as it is in a word-processing program. Instead it is displayed in the page by an HTML command which instructs the browser how it should be displayed. The image remains as a separate file, typically a GIF or JPEG.

To insert an image on your page:

1. Place the cursor where you want the image to appear.
2. On the **Insert bar** click on the **Image** button under the Common tab.
   Or
   Go to **Insert > Image (Ctrl+Alt+I / Cmd+Option+I)**.
3. In the **Select Image** dialog box (Figure 4.1) browse to and select your image.

The image will appear selected in your page and the image options will be displayed in the Property inspector (Figure 4.2).

Image properties

■ **Name**. It is important to name your image if you want to use the image with a JavaScript behaviour, such as a mouse rollover (more on rollovers later in this chapter and JavaScript will be further explained in Chapter 10: Working with behaviours).

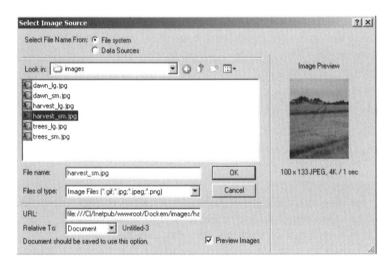

Figure 4.1 Select Image window.

If you are waiting on the final graphics for a page but still want to work on the layout, you can use an image 'placeholder' to mark the image position. In the Common tab of the Insert bar, click on the Image Placeholder button > Define the image and click OK. When you are ready you insert the final image by double-clicking on the placeholder and browsing to your image.

Figure 4.2 Image properties.

- **Width and height**. Displays the dimensions (in pixels) of the image. Dreamweaver inserts the dimensions automatically, which improves the download time of your page.

- **Reset Size**. Use to reset the original (or true) width and height of your image if you have changed them.

- **Src**. Indicates where the graphic is located in the site files.

- **Link**. Displays the URL of a linked graphic.

- **Align**. Relates to the alignment of an image to text or other objects in the same line.

- **Alt**. The text alternative to a graphic – for users with images turned off in their browser or for speech-synthesised browsers for the visually impaired. Some search engines also read and index Alt text. Using Microsoft Internet Explorer on a PC you will notice that the Alt text also appears in a yellow box when the user rolls over an image. Be aware that this does not appear on a Mac.

- **V Space and H Space**. Inserts transparent space around your image on the vertical and horizontal.

- **Target**. If your image is a link the target will specify which window or frame the linked page should open in (see Chapter 6: Working with frames).

- **Low Src**. If your image is large and going to take a while to download you can specify another image (of the same dimensions) to download first. It could be, for instance, a black and white, low-resolution version of your image. Use Low Src sparingly as every extra graphic will add to the page's overall download time.

- **Border**. If an image is a link it may be displayed in the browser with a border around it (just as linked text appears underlined). Dreamweaver sets a default value of 0 when an image is linked – because most of the time you won't want a border to appear.

- **Map**. Is where you name and create an image map (see later in this chapter: Linking with image maps).

- **Edit**. Use the Edit button to open a graphics program, if available, to edit an image.

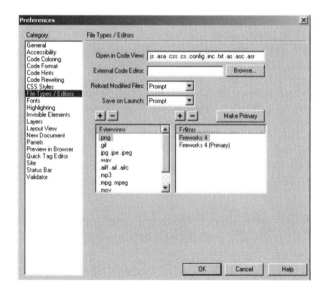

To set up an image-editing program to work with Dreamweaver:

1. *Go to* **Edit > Preferences**.
2. *Select* **File Types/Editors** *from the Category list.*
3. *In the Extensions dialog box (Figure 4.3) highlight a graphics extension, such as GIF or JPEG, and above the Editors box click the* **plus (+)** *button to navigate to and select your preferred graphics program.*

Figure 4.3 Image editing preferences.

*If you want the image to retain its proportions as you resize it, hold down the **shift** key while you drag from the corner handle.*

The Alignment drop-down menu is a bit different to the normal sort of alignment you may be used to, so to simply align an image on the page, say to centre it, use the three alignment buttons at the bottom right of the Property inspector.

Resizing an image

Once you have inserted an image in Dreamweaver it will appear selected with resize handles (the black boxes on the bottom right corner and edges). You can drag these handles to resize it (though if an image needs resizing it is usually best to do this in a graphics package). In some cases, resizing may be useful for playing around with the page format or if you are drastically pressed for time.

To resize an image:

Select the graphic and use the resize handles to reduce or enlarge the image.

Or

Select the graphic and type new dimensions into the width (**W**) and height (**H**) boxes in the **Property inspector**.

To revert the graphic to its original (or true) dimensions, click on the **Reset Size** button in the bottom right corner of the **Property inspector**.

Image alignment

When you use the Alignment drop-down menu in the Property inspector, the options relate to the image 'in-line', that is, in relation to text or other objects in the same line.

To experiment with in-line alignment, insert an image on a page and type some text next to it. Select the image and apply alignment options to it. The options are:

- **Default**. Usually the same as baseline.

- **Baseline**. Aligns the image to the text baseline. The baseline is the line of the text which the descenders drop below (descenders are the downward tails in letters such as 'p' or 'g').

- **Top**. Aligns text with the top of the image.

- **Middle**. Aligns the middle of the image with the text baseline.

- **Bottom**. Aligns the bottom of the image and the selected object.

- **Text top**. Aligns the tallest text character with the top of the image.

- **Absolute middle**. Aligns the middle of the image with the middle of the text.

- **Absolute bottom**. Aligns the image to the bottom of the text including the descenders.

- **Left**. Aligns the image with the left of the page and places text or other objects to its right.

- **Right**. Aligns the image with the right of the page and places text or other objects to its left.

Creating links

Linking is really the essence of HTML and navigating the World Wide Web. With Dreamweaver you can link between pages, jump between particular items on the same page, link to other Websites, and set up email links. A link is written in HTML using the anchor tag <A> and the attribute HREF (which stands for Hypertext Reference).

There are two types of links commonly used on the Web: absolute links and relative links. Absolute links are generally used to link to other Websites as they give the full, or absolute, location of the site being linked to, ie: http://www.site-name.com. Relative links are used to link between pages in a Website, and do not use the absolute location of a file, but use the location of a file being linked *to* in relation to the page *from* which the link is made. For example, if your page is in a folder named **clients** and you want to link to a page that sits in another folder named **staff**, the link may look something like '**../staff/filename.html**'. What the '**../**' does is tell the browser to come out of the **clients** folder (or come up a level) and then directs it to go into the **staff** folder and locate the new page. If your pages were in the same folder then all that would need to be written in the link would be the file name 'filename.html'.

Both text and images can be made into links and the process is the same because Dreamweaver treats them both as page objects.

Linking from one page to another

1. Highlight the text or *image* that you want to make into a link.

2. In the **Property inspector** go to the right of the Link box and click on the **Folder** icon to open the Select File window (Figure 4.4).

3. Browse and select the page you want to link to.

4. The link won't actually work in Dreamweaver so you'll need to preview in the browser to check that it works.

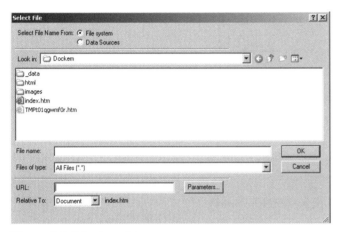

Figure 4.4 Selecting a link.

When an image is made into a link the browser will, by default, insert a border around the image indicating that it is a link (just as it displays linked text as underlined). You may notice that Dreamweaver automatically gives a linked image a border value of '0' to turn off the default border. If you want the border to appear around the image insert a value (in pixels) in the Property inspector.

Linking to another Website

1. Highlight the text or image that you want to make into a link.

2. In the **Link** box in the **Property inspector** type in the URL (or address) of the Website you want to link to. When you type in the address make sure you insert the full address, including the **http** (Hypertext Transfer Protocol) at the beginning, for example: http://www.website.com

Creating an email link

1. Go to the **Insert** bar and click on the **Insert E-Mail Link** button.

2. In the dialog box (Figure 4.5) type in the text you want to appear underlined on the page – this can be the email address or other text – and type in the email address.

*If you link to another Website and want it to open up in a new browser window, type in the URL and then go to the **Target** box to the right of the Link box in the Property inspector and choose **blank** from the drop-down menu. Test it in the browser to see it in action!*

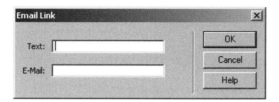

Figure 4.5 Inserting an email link.

You will see that the email address now appears in the Property inspector Link box preceded by the command 'mailto:'.

Linking to items within a page (anchor links)

You can set up a list of links at the top of a page that allows users to click directly to items in that page, rather than having to scroll down, or click to other pages. These links are set up by creating anchor points on a page (the places where you want a user to go *to*) and then creating links that take the user to those points.

To set up a system of anchor links on a page you first need to insert the anchor point (known as a Named Anchor) and then create the link to it.

To set up a named anchor in your document:

1. Go to the place where you want the user to go to.
2. Go to the **Insert bar** and select **Named Anchor**, under the **Common** tab.
3. Type in a name (Figure 4.6).

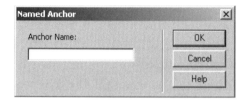

Figure 4.6 The Named Anchor window.

To link to a named anchor in the same page:

1. Select the text or image you want to make into a link.

2. In the Property inspector **Link** box type in a hash symbol, then the name of the link. For example, if the anchor name is 'accounts' the link would be '#accounts'.

   Or

   In the Property inspector click on the **Point to File** icon and drag the pointer to the named anchor (Figure 4.7).

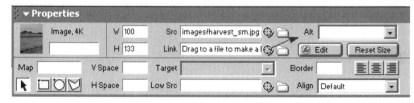

Figure 4.7 Using the Point to File tool.

Important: Anchor names should be one word – no spaces.

*When you insert a named anchor, because it is operating 'behind the scenes', you will probably see a Dreamweaver **Invisible Element** icon appear on the page. Dreamweaver displays this to indicate that the anchor is there and allows you to change the anchor name by clicking on it. To turn invisible elements on or off go to **Edit > Preferences**. Choose the **Invisible Elements** category and make your changes.*

Linking to an anchor in another page

You can link to an anchor in another page following a similar method as described above.

1. Select the text or image you want to make into a link.

2. In the **Property inspector** use the **Folder** icon to select the file that contains the Named Anchor.

3. In the Link box type in the hash symbol (#) followed by the anchor name directly after the filename. For example, if the anchor name is 'accounts' and it's in the clients page (clients.html), the link would look like 'clients.html#accounts'.

Or

Open the page where you want to link to and use the **Point to File** icon to point to the anchor in the second page.

Linking using jump menus

A jump menu is a drop-down menu of links to other pages or Websites (Figure 4.8). It is a great way to save space on a page if you have a long list of pages to link to. For instance, if you wanted to create links to city sites around the world a jump menu would be ideal.

Figure 4.8 A sample jump menu.

To insert a jump menu:

1. Go to the **Insert** bar and select the **Forms** tab.
2. Select the **Jump Menu** button.

    Or

    Go to **Insert > Form Objects > Jump Menu**.

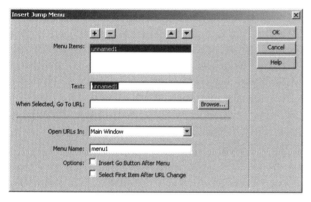

Figure 4.9 The Jump Menu window.

3. In the **Insert Jump Menu** dialog box (Figure 4.9) go to the Text box and type in the name you want to appear in the menu, i.e. one of your Menu items.

A jump menu is created using a form element and a behaviour. Before trying to create a jump menu you may want to have a look at Chapter 7: Creating forms and Chapter 10: Working with behaviours.

4. In the URL field use the **Browse** button to navigate to and select the file you want to link to, or type in the URL of a Website.

5. To add your next menu item and URL, click on the **plus (+)** button situated above the Menu Items box. Continue like this with each item to make your menu. Use the up and down arrow buttons above the Menu Items box to change the order of your menu items.

6. Choose your options (which apply to the whole menu, not to individual items).

Options:

Insert Go Button After Menu: When someone selects an item on a jump menu they immediately go to it – which makes you wonder why they would need a 'Go' button. The button is used if the item at the top of your jump menu is one of your link options, which means that if they want to choose it they need a Go button. Go buttons are also useful, because once a user has selected an item and returns to the page or is working within a frameset, the Go button will enable them to select that same link again.

Select First Item After URL Change: Check this box if you want to give your user some instructions in the first item, such as Select City, and want that item to always appear visible when the user returns to the page after previously following a link.

7. Click on **OK** and test your menu in the browser.

Editing jump menus

As I mentioned before, jump menus are not all that straightforward. To edit a jump menu you can make some changes in the Property inspector but to access all options you need to edit the menu using the Behaviors panel. You may want to learn about behaviours first in Chapter 10.

Figure 4.10 The Jump Menu Behaviors.

1. Select the jump menu you want to open.
2. Open the **Behaviors** panel, found in the Design panel group, and the jump menu will appear as an action attached to the **onChange** event (Figure 4.10).
3. Double-click on the name **Jump Menu** in the Actions column.
4. Make your changes in the dialog box.

Linking with image maps

An image map is an image that has 'hotspots', or multiple links, attached to it. For example, if you had an image that was an actual map and you wanted to link place names to different pages in your site, you could use an image map to set up links, or hotspots, around the place names on the map.

Try not to create your hotspots too close to each other as it may confuse the user as to which link they are selecting.

To create an image map:

1. Select the image you want to attach hotspots to.

2. In the **Property inspector** type a name for the map in the **Map name** box (Figure 4.11).

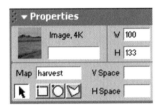

Figure 4.11 Naming an image map.

3. Click on a hotspot shape icon, then click on the image and drag to create a hotspot. The Property inspector will now display the **Image Map** options (Figure 4.12).

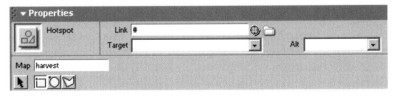

Figure 4.12 Image Map options.

4. In the Property inspector use the **Folder** icon to navigate to and select a file to link to.

5. Type in some **Alt text** for the link and select a **Target** if it is appropriate.

6. Repeat steps 3–5 to create further hotspots.

To move a hotspot:

Click on the hotspot you want to move and drag the mouse or use the arrow keys to reposition.

Creating a simple mouse rollover

A mouse rollover is when the user passes the mouse over an image and the image changes, for example text in a button might change colour. To create a rollover you need two images: one is the primary image, the one that is visible when the page loads up, and the other is the rollover image.

To insert a mouse rollover:

1. In the **Insert** bar, under the **Common** tab select the **Rollover Image** button.

2. In the window select the **Original Image** and the **Rollover Image**.

3. Select the **URL** or page that you want to link to and type in some Alt text.

4. Click **OK**.

Make sure your rollover images are the same size. The primary image will always set your size, so if the rollover image is larger or smaller it will stretch or shrink to fit the area.

Designing with tables

The Dreamweaver table tools

Using Layout View

Creating tables in Standard View

Importing tables into Dreamweaver

Tables are used extensively on the Web to set up the layout for pages. You may have already noticed that the layout techniques discussed so far in this guide are fairly basic: left, centre and right alignment, paragraph indents and so on. Not much room to manoeuvre and certainly very little control over the look of your page – which is where tables come in handy.

Tables enable you to arrange text and graphics both horizontally (in rows) and vertically (in columns), to merge cells across rows and columns, to set background colours for whole tables and for individual cells, and to align content within those cells. Figure 5.1 is designed to illustrate how a simple table can be used to set the layout for a Web page. Note that there is a border around the table. Typically you would have table borders hidden on the page, which is the default setting in Dreamweaver.

It is definitely worth familiarising yourself with the HTML format of tables. The three main tags to recognise are: for a table <TABLE>, for a table row <TR> and for a table cell <TD> – which stands for table data.

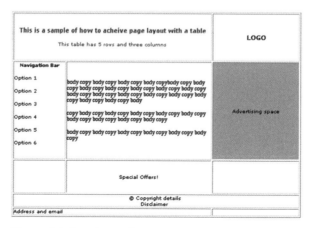

Figure 5.1 Sample page layout.

Although they are commonly used, tables can be tricky to work with and pretty frustrating. Time, patience and practice are what you need – so don't get discouraged early if your table doesn't display exactly as it should. It will … eventually!

The Dreamweaver table tools

There are two ways of inserting and formatting tables in Dreamweaver, which are described below:

1. **Using Layout View**. In Layout View you can draw table cells on a page by dragging the mouse and modify their size using resize handles.

2. **Using Standard View (Insert > Table)**. This is the more 'traditional' way of creating a table that you may have seen if you have used previous versions of Dreamweaver. It is useful if you are creating a table that is very simple in structure, in particular for inserting tabular data, or in other circumstances, where you have a very clear idea of how your content fits in columns and rows.

It is worth getting to know both methods as you will find them equally useful in different situations.

Using Layout View

To use Layout View you need to change from Standard View to Layout View found under the Layout tab on the **Insert** bar (Figure 5.2).

Drawing table cells

Choose the **Draw Layout Cell** button and drag the mouse in the document window. You don't have to draw a table *before* drawing a table cell, as Dreamweaver will automatically create one around a new cell.

If you find working with tables just too difficult, you can always lay out your page using layers – which lets you drag content around the page – and then convert the layers to tables … but that'll come later (see Chapter 9: Advanced formatting using layers and timelines).

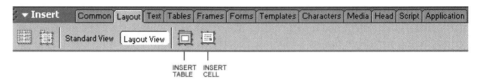

Figure 5.2 Layout View options.

A few things to notice once you have drawn a cell (Figure 5.3):

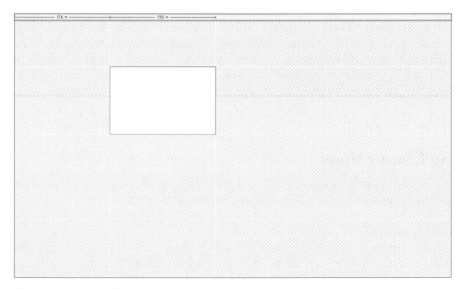

Figure 5.3 A cell within a table.

1. The table cell is white and surrounded by a blue outline. When you move the mouse over the outline it will appear highlighted (in red) which indicates you can select the cell.

2. The surrounding table is drawn in grey and has a green outline. The grey boxes in the table are the other rows and columns, which help to position the cell on the page.

3. At the top of the column that is holding the cell a width (in pixels) should be displayed. You may also have another column, drawn in grey but displaying a width, if you drew the original cell in from the left side of the page.

To draw additional cells, you may need to click back on the **Draw Layout Cell** button, or hold down the **Ctrl/Cmd** key when you drag a cell and you will then be able to draw one after another.

Adding content to a table cell

You can add text, images and – well – just about anything to a table, in both Page Layout mode and Standard mode. Type text directly into a table cell and use the Property inspector to format it. Insert images just as you would on a normal page.

You can also copy and paste, and drag and drop images and text from outside the table or between cells in the table.

Table and cell options in Page Layout

The options available in Page Layout will vary in the Property inspector depending on whether you have the entire table selected or a single cell (Figure 5.4).

You may find it difficult to draw a layout table when there is other content already on the page. Try resizing the document window to provide extra white space in which to draw the table.

Options for table layout

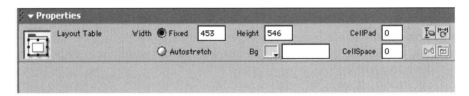

Figure 5.4 Table Layout options.

- **Width and Height**. Width is displayed with two options: one is set in pixels, the other is Autostretch which is described below.
- **Bg**. Sets the background colour for the table.
- **CellPad**. Adds space around text or objects *within* each of the table cells.
- **CellSpace**. Adds space *between* table cells rather than within them.
- **Clear row heights button**. Clears all set heights in the table – which is useful once you have added content to your page as it leaves the height flexible for text (which can change size on different monitors).
- **Make cell widths consistent button**. Forces cell widths to be consistent with content and is described in more detail below.
- **Remove all spacers**. Removes any spacer images that have been inserted in the table.
- **Remove nesting**. Makes a nested table into cells of the parent table.

Options for cell layout

The options for a cell layout are the same as a table for width, height and background colour (Figure 5.5). Other options particular to a cell are:

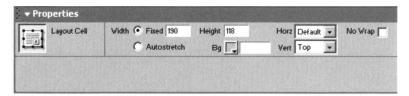

Figure 5.5 Cell layout options.

- **Horz**. Horizontally aligns the content of a cell – left, centre or right.
- **Vert**. Vertically aligns the content of a cell – top, middle, bottom or baseline.
- **No Wrap**. If you select **No Wrap** a cell will widen as you type into it, rather than wrap text which forces the height of the cell to increase.

Changing the width of a cell or column

When you change the width of a cell remember that it will affect the entire column. You can set table cells to a fixed width (in pixels) or use what is known as 'Autostretch', which allows the cell to grow and shrink to fit the user's browser window. The Autostretch option is useful when you have, for instance, a left-hand column containing site navigation, which you would like to keep a fixed width, and a right-hand column containing content that you would like to have flexible.

To change the width of a cell or column:

1. Select the cell by highlighting and clicking on the blue outline around the cell. You will notice that the resize handles appear (Figure 5.6).

Have a look at different Websites and see how their tables are set up. Does the page expand to fit when you change your browser window? Take a look at www.amazon.co.uk and notice which columns use a set width and which are set to Autostretch.

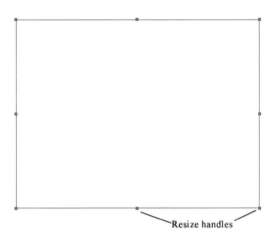

Figure 5.6 Cell resize handles.

2. Drag using the resize handles.

Or

For a more precise change, go to the **Property inspector** and change the width value.

To set a cell to Autostretch:

1. Select the cell by clicking on the blue outline around the cell.

2. Choose the **Autostretch** option in the **Property inspector**.

You can only have one column in a table set to Autostretch.

Or

1. Click on the number at the top of the column.
2. Choose **Make Column Autostretch**.

Making cells and content consistent widths

Sometimes you may find that you've created a table cell with a set width, then inserted an image that is larger than that width. When this happens the width value at the top of the column will display two numbers: the first is the original width of the cell and the second (in brackets) is the width of the image. To ensure the stability of the table, table cells should be at *least* the same width as the image.

To change the original cell width to fit the image:

1. Click on the width values at the top of the column.
2. Choose **Make Widths Consistent** from the drop-down menu.

What is the spacer image?

The first time that you choose to make a column Autostretch you will be asked if you want to create a spacer image. 'Well, maybe,' you answer 'but, what is it and what does it do?' The spacer image is a small transparent GIF (1 pixel × 1 pixel) that can be 'stretched' horizontally or vertically to set a table cell's width and/or height. Once the image (spacer) width or height is set, a table cell is forced to be at least that size, thus establishing a set area for your content.

Nesting tables

You can create a new table within an existing table to achieve more complex page designs and to keep particular areas of content layout separate from the rest of the table. This is what is known as 'nesting' tables (Figure 5.7).

You only need one spacer image in your site files because, like any other graphic, it can be used over and over again.

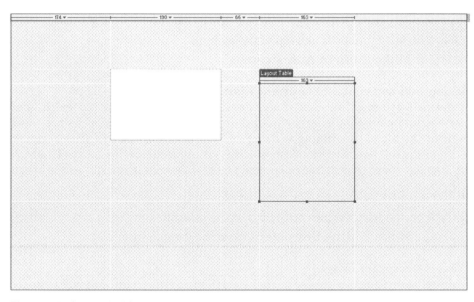

Figure 5.7 A nested table.

You may find it easier to create the smaller (nested) table first, then simply copy and paste, or drag it into the parent table cell – using the Standard View mode.

To nest a table:

1. Create a table into which you are going to nest another table.
2. Make sure the area where you want to draw the table is grey, as you can't nest a table inside an existing table cell – which would appear white.
3. Drag to create the nested table.
4. You can then create layout cells in either of the tables.

Creating tables in Standard View

Once you have created the layout of your page, you may prefer to switch to Standard View to continue working as you'll find that there are several more formatting options available. You can also create a table from the outset in Standard View, which may be faster than Layout View if you have a clear idea of the structure of your rows and columns and if you are inserting tabular data.

Inserting a table

1. Place your cursor where you want the table to appear.

2. In the **Layout** tab of the **Insert** bar, select Standard View.

3. Click on the **Insert** button.

    Or

    Go to **Insert > Table**.

4. In the dialog box (Figure 5.8) type in the number of rows and columns, the width of the table (in pixels or as a percentage of the browser window), Cell Padding and Cell Spacing – which are set to '0' as a default value – and the size of the table border – set to a default value of '1'.

When you insert further tables, the table dialog box will display your previous table settings.

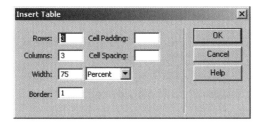

Figure 5.8 The Insert Table window.

5. Click on **OK** and a table will appear in your page.

Selecting a table
You can select a table in several ways:

- Click on the outer border of the table.
- Place the cursor in the table and select the <TABLE> tag in the tag selector area along the bottom of the document window (Figure 5.9).

Figure 5.9 The Tag Selector.

When a table is selected it will appear highlighted with resize handles.

Additional table properties
Once you have inserted a table its properties will appear in the **Property inspector** (Figure 5.10). The options are similar to those described in Page Layout but you no longer have the option of making a cell Autostretch, although you have some additional options, which are described below.

- **Table ID**. An identifying name for the table.
- **Align**. Aligns the table within the browser window (left, right, or centre). Tables are always left-aligned, by default, in a Web browser.
- **Border**. Sets a border around your table and cells. You may find it easier to create a table with a border value of 1, then turn the border off later by setting the border value to 0.

The Brdr Color may display differently in Netscape and in Microsoft Internet Explorer. Be sure to test all your work in the different browsers and platforms.

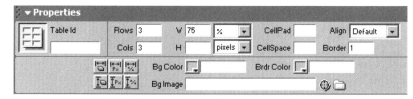

Figure 5.10 Standard View table properties.

- **Clear height (H) and width (W) buttons**. Clears all set heights and widths of the table and its columns and rows.
- **Convert to pixels or percentages buttons**. Converts the table width or height to pixels or percentages.
- **Bg Image**. Just as you can for a page, you can set a background image for a table, which will automatically tile, or repeat.
- **Bg Color**. Sets the background colour for the table.
- **Brdr Color**. Sets the border colour for the entire table.

Working with table cells

When you place your cursor in a table cell, in the Property inspector your normal text formatting options will appear in the top half and your cell properties will appear in the bottom half (Figure 5.11).

Formatting individual cells

You can add many formatting options to individual cells, or to rows and columns. In the Property inspector the options you have are:

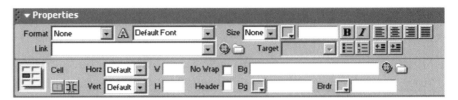

Figure 5.11 Standard View table cell properties.

■ **Width (W) and Height (H)**. To force a width (which will affect the whole column) or height (which will affect the row) in a cell using pixels or percentages.

■ **Horizontal (Horz) and Vertical (Vert) alignment**. Aligns objects and text within a cell.

■ **No Wrap**. If you select 'No Wrap' a cell will widen as you type into it.

■ **Header**. Use this option if you want to use a default table header text, which will be bold and centred.

You also have the option to add background images, colours and border colours to the cell.

Working with rows and columns

You can format multiple cells by selecting rows and columns and using the same formatting options as described for table cells.

Formatting rows and columns

1. Select the row or column by clicking in a table cell and dragging across the entire row or column.

2. Make your changes in the **Property inspector**.

Adding rows and columns

To insert a row or column in the table:

1. Place the cursor in the cell where you want the new row or column.

2. Go to **Modify > Table > Insert Rows or Columns.**

3. In the dialog box choose the number and position of the rows or columns you want to insert (Figure 5.12).

*You can quickly add a row to the bottom of your table by clicking in the bottom right cell and using the **Tab** key.*

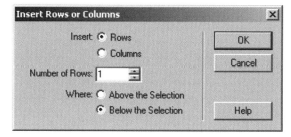

Figure 5.12 Inserting rows or columns.

Deleting rows and columns

1. Place the cursor in the row or column you want to delete.

2. Go to **Modify > Tables > Delete Row or Delete Column.**

Merging and splitting cells

Half the fun of working with tables is being able to merge multiple table cells. In HTML this is referred to as spanning, that is, two cells are merged so that the new cell spans two columns (Figure 5.13).

This cell spans the other three columns		

Figure 5.13 Spanning columns.

To merge cells:

1. Click in the first cell and drag the mouse across, up or down to select multiple cells.
2. Click on the **Merge Selected Cells** button at the bottom left of the **Property inspector**.

To split cells:

1. Place the cursor in the merged cell you want to split.
2. Click on the **Split Cells** button (next to the **Merge** button) in the **Property inspector**.
3. In the dialog box you will be asked to split the cells to the original number or you can reduce or increase the number of cells.

Resizing a table

To resize a table:

- Select the table and type in new dimensions in the **Property inspector**.

    Or

- Use the resize handles to drag your table to the left, down or out diagonally.

To change the width of a column:

- Drag the border to the right of the column.

    Or

- Select the column and type in a width in the **Property inspector**.

To change the height of a row:

- Drag the lower border of the row.

    Or

- Select the row and type in a height in the **Property inspector**.

Importing tables into Dreamweaver

You can use data created in other programs, such as Microsoft Excel, and import it directly into a table. You must save the data with a delimiter, for example a tab, and then use the import command in Dreamweaver.

To import data saved with a delimiter:

1. Go to **File > Import > Tabular Data** (Figure 5.14).

If you choose to increase the number of cells, that is, to more than there were originally, Dreamweaver will automatically add extra columns to your table to accommodate the new cells. You can use the Split Cells button on any cells, not just merged ones.

If you have grid-style data to go into a table you can use one of the pre-set table layouts that come with Dreamweaver MX. To access the pre-set tables go to Commands > Format Table. Select your format and colours and click OK.

*You can use the '**Save as HTML**' option in Microsoft Excel, but you will find that, as in Microsoft Word, the HTML produced is code heavy and you will get a much cleaner result by following the instructions here. It is always worth testing different methods if the results are not exactly as you predicted.*

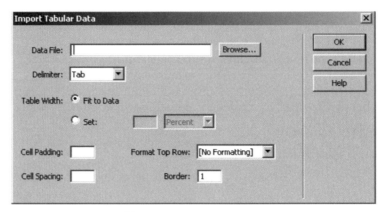

Figure 5.14 Importing Tabular Data.

2. In the dialog box navigate to and select the data file to import.

3. Select the delimiter that the table was saved with.

4. Fill in the table formatting options.

Working with frames

Understanding frames and the frameset

Creating a frameset

Adding content to frame pages

Saving a frameset and frame pages

Formatting a frameset

Formatting individual frames

Linking between pages in a frameset

Creating a nested frameset

Adding existing pages to a frameset

NoFrames Content: what's that?

6

Using frames allows you to divide your Web page into different 'windows' that display different HTML pages at the same time. For instance, you may have one frame displaying navigation on the left side of the page, and another frame displaying page content on the right hand area (Figure 6.1). You can link between pages in a frames structure and set how you want each frame to display, for instance, with scroll bars, borders and margins.

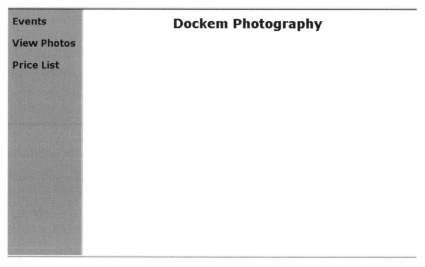

Figure 6.1 Sample two-column frameset.

Understanding frames and the frameset

When you create a site in frames, for example the page shown in Figure 6.1, you are essentially creating three pages:

1. The navigation page, which is displayed in a frame on the left.
2. The contents page, which is displayed in a frame on the right.
3. The frameset page, which is not actually visible but contains the instructions for the frames that contain your two pages, for instance the width or height of the two frames.

In Dreamweaver you don't need to create these pages separately. You simply split your page into frames, each of which contains a page, edit each page within its frame, then save each of the pages, starting with the frameset, which is the invisible instructions page.

Just a word of caution – frames cause many Web developers to start frothing at the mouth and it's important for you to know why. Because your page is embedded in a frameset, visitors to your site may find it difficult to add a particular page to their favourites and to print a page. Search engines can also have a hard time finding and indexing all of your pages. Have a look at different sites on the Web to see who's using frames and who's not.

Creating a frameset

Before you start creating frames turn on the **Frame Borders** option in the document window and open up the **Frames** panel to make it easy to see what you are doing and what your options are.

It is worth saving your frameset and frames pages early on and following the instructions below carefully – it is easy to get a bit confused!

Figure 6.2 The Frames panel.

- To turn on Frame Borders go to **View > Visual Aids > Frame Borders**.
- To open the Frames panel go to the **Advanced Layout** panel group and select the **Frames** tab (Figure 6.2).

You can create a frameset using several different methods, which are described below.

To create a frameset:

Hold down the **Alt/Option** key and drag a **Frame Border** from the edge of the document window.

Or

1. Go to the **Insert** bar and select the **Frames** tab.
2. Click on the format you prefer in the **Frames** menu (Figure 6.3).

Figure 6.3 Frames layout options.

Or

Go to **Modify > Frameset > Split Frame Left, Right, Up or Down**.

To change the size of the frames you have created, move the mouse over the Frame Border in the document window and when the double arrow appears drag the border. To make more specific changes to frame dimensions see the section: Formatting a frameset.

Adding content to frame pages

Remember that each frame in your frameset is actually a different Web page. You can therefore type directly into that frame, edit content, set page properties and so on – just as you would in a normal page.

To create pages from within the frameset:

1. Create your frameset as described previously.
2. Add content such as text and images to each frame and set your page properties.

When you're creating a frameset for the first time, you'll probably find it easier to grasp the concepts and avoid major pitfalls if you keep the structure nice and simple: two frames, either columns or rows. When you are starting it's easy to get a bit confused – particularly with frame naming, saving and linking!

The frameset tag in HTML is <FRAMESET> and the <FRAME> tag defines the frame areas. It's worth having a look at the code for different framesets on the Web to see how different framesets are brought together.

When you are saving your pages watch the window carefully so you are certain you are saving the page you think you are saving.

Saving a frameset and frame pages

The simplest and safest way to save your frame pages and the frameset is to use the **Save All Frames** option, which lets Dreamweaver do all the hard work and walks you through the process.

Choose **File > Save All**.

Dreamweaver will prompt you to save the frameset first (you will see that the outer border of the document window is highlighted) and then prompt for each of your frame pages. Each frame will be highlighted in the document window to let you know which one you are saving.

Formatting a frameset

When you are working with frames there are certain properties you set that relate to the frameset page, and others you set for each frame.

The properties to set for the frameset are the size of the borders in the frameset and the dimensions of the columns or rows of each frame (Figure 6.4).

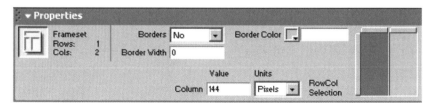

Figure 6.4 The Frameset Properties.

To change the properties for the frameset:

1. Select the frameset by either:

   Clicking on the outside border in the **Frames** panel.

   Or

   Clicking on a visible border between two frames in the document window.

2. In the Property inspector choose **Borders**, **Border widths** and **Border colors**.

Change the width and/or height of a frame

When you are setting frame sizes you would normally have one frame with a fixed size, for example, the navigation frame, and the other a variable size, to enlarge and contract to fit the browser window (like having an 'Autostretch' column in a table). Make sure, when you are setting frame sizes in the Property inspector, that you select a relative size for the frame you want to be flexible.

1. Select the frameset using either of the methods described above.

2. In the **Property inspector**, change the width and height of another frame by clicking in the frame area in the **RowCol Selection** box. You will notice that the dimensions will display whichever frame you have selected.

Formatting individual frames

To display individual frame options in the Property inspector click on a frame area in the Frames panel (Figure 6.5).

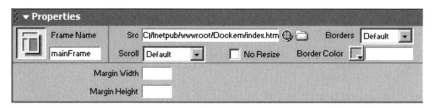

Figure 6.5 Frame Properties.

*To turn Borders off in your frameset, and to make sure it applies across both browsers, set Borders to **No** in the **Frames Properties** and also in the **Frameset Properties**.*

- **Frame Name**. It is important to name a frame to enable links to work properly within the frames structure (see the section in this chapter Linking between pages in a frameset). When you name your frames always use one word, underscores and numbers. No hyphens, periods or spaces should be used.

- **Scroll**. You can set whether you want scroll bars to appear in your frame. Most browsers default to **Auto** and will display scroll bars if the size of the content requires them.

- **No Resize**. Ensures that users cannot change the display of your frames in the browser window – that is, if you have visible borders around your frames.

- **Borders**. Sets the border for that frame and overrides border settings for the frameset.

- **Border Color**. Sets the colour for all the borders around the selected frame. As with the Borders properties, this will override a border colour defined in the frameset.

■ **Margin Width**. Sets space (in pixels) to the left and right of the frame content.

■ **Margin Height**. Sets space (in pixels) at the top and bottom of the frame content.

Linking between pages in a frameset

To link between pages in a frameset you need to specify which frame you would like a linked page to open up in. If you create a link in a frames page, without targeting a particular frame, your new page will open up in the same frame – try it … I bet it's not the result you were after!

To target a particular frame you must first make sure that you have named all of the frames in the frameset.

To make the link between frames:

1. Select the text or object that you want to make into a link.

2. In the **Property inspector**, create a link to another page or site as you would normally.

3. From the **Target** drop-down menu (Figure 6.6), select the frame for the new document to open in. Frame names should automatically appear after the default options in the **Target** drop-down menu. The default frameset target options are:

■ **_blank** – Opens the linked page in a new browser window (out of the frameset).

■ **_parent** – In a nested frameset this target opens the linked page in the frame that holds the nested frameset.

Figure 6.6 Selecting a frame target.

- **_self** – Opens the linked page in the frame where the link sits.
- **_top** – Opens the linked page in the whole browser window (the frameset disappears).

Creating a nested frameset

A nested frameset splits one frame into two or more frames (Figure 6.7).

To nest a new frameset, place your cursor in the frame you want to split then choose one of the options described earlier in Creating a frameset.

Save the new frameset and frames page using the **Save all** option.

Adding existing pages to a frameset

You can always bring existing HTML pages into a frameset. To do so, split the page into the frames you require, then:

1. In the **Frames** panel, select the frame where you want the page to appear.
2. In the **Property inspector** click on the **Source File Folder** icon and browse to and select the file you want to display in the frame.

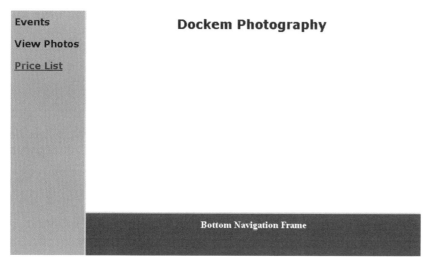

Figure 6.7 Sample of a nested frameset.

Or

1. Click on the frame area in the document window.

2. Go to **File > Open in Frame** and browse to and select the file you want to display in the frame.

3. If the frames pages were all pre-existing, to save the new frameset, go to **File > Save frameset**.

Remember that you are dealing with different entities here. You have the frameset, which is the HTML file that holds all the information about the frames – whether the pages are displayed as columns or rows, their dimensions, scrolling options, the page source files, frame names and so on. And then you have the individual pages that are displayed in each of the frames.

NoFrames Content: what's that?

NoFrames Content enables users with older and text-based browsers that do not support frames to view your site. The purpose of NoFrames Content is to allow those users to navigate through and view your site, therefore, the most important elements to include in NoFrames are links to your other pages and contact details where appropriate.

Your NoFrames Content will only appear to users who can't view frames, and otherwise will not be displayed.

To add NoFrames Content to a frameset document:

*Adding links to your pages in **NoFrames Content** can also help search engines to navigate and index your site.*

1. Go to **Modify > Frameset > Edit NoFrames Content**.
2. In the **NoFrames** window create the **NoFrames Content** as you would any other page with some explanatory text and links.
3. Go to **Modify > Frameset > Edit NoFrames Content** to return to your document.

Creating forms

7

Creating a form

Understanding form objects

Using form objects

Some useful references

Forms are used to enable user interactivity and to collect information, for instance you can use forms to set up a guestbook on your site or to request that users fill in a questionnaire. Forms are made up of form 'objects' such as text boxes, which the user types into directly, and a form 'action' which sends the information to be processed when the user hits the Submit button.

To enable form processing, for example to have questionnaire data sent to you as an email, you need to set up some sort of script or form 'handler'. The type of script used is known as a CGI, or Common Gateway Interface, script, and is usually written in a programming language such as Perl.

'So how do you do that?' you ask. Well, there is no straightforward answer, but the first thing you should do if you are considering using an interactive form on your site is to talk to whoever is hosting your site. You need to check that they support CGI and ask whether they have any available scripts on the server that you may use. If they do support CGI, but have no scripts, there are plenty of free scripts available on the Web and most come with instructions to help you set them up. See the end of this chapter for some useful CGI references.

The diagram below shows how form data is processed and sent (Figure 7.1).

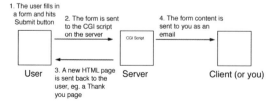

Figure 7.1 Submitting form data.

Creating a form

1. Go to the **Insert** bar and select the **Forms** tab (Figure 7.2).

Figure 7.2 Forms object buttons.

2. Select the **Insert Form** button. A rectangular box with a red dotted outline will appear in the document window to indicate that you are working within a form.

3. In the **Property inspector** fill in the form properties, which are:

   Name. Name the form to make it possible to process and control the form with scripts.

   Action. Enter a link to the script that will process the form – something you can only do once you've got a handle on setting up the CGI script.

   Method. Choose how the form is to be handled. Generally this can be left as the default which is GET, but note that the GET method is not secure, so if you were processing anything confidential such as credit card details, it would be appropriate to use the POST method. Again, you will need to discuss the form method with your host server. Figure 7.3 shows a sample form.

   Target. Is used if the form is going to be sending a new HTML page back to the user from within a frameset. See the previous chapter for an explanation of the Target options.

   Enctype. Select an encryption from the drop-down menu. If you want users to send file information, for instance if you are asking them to attach a CV, select the multipart/ formdata option.

If you miss out on this first step and insert a form object directly on to the page, Dreamweaver will automatically insert the <FORM> tag around the object. Use the tag selector at the bottom of the Document window to select the form and set up the Form Properties.

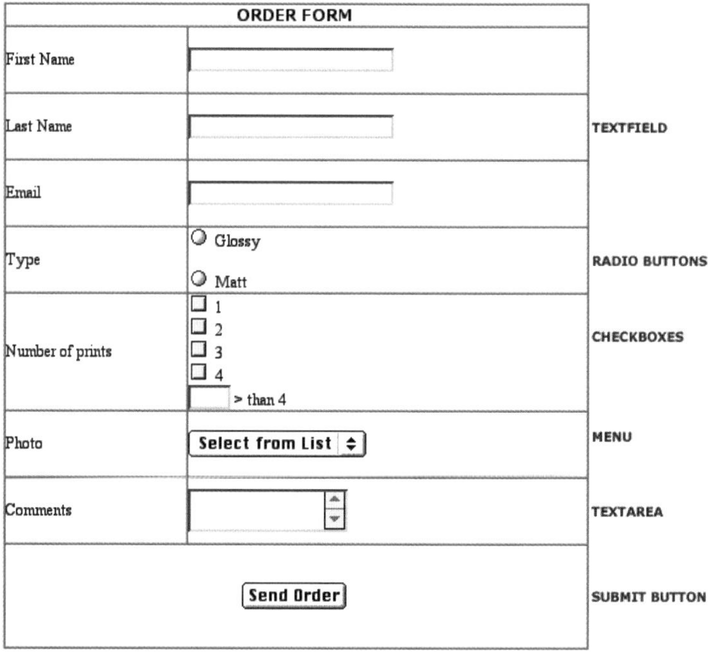

Figure 7.3 Sample form.

Understanding form objects

Listed below are all of the form objects you can use, also known as form 'widgets'. All form objects have a name and many have an associated value. The name is the name of the particular question being asked, for example, email address, comments or preferences. When the user types in a response, as is the case with a text field, the response becomes the form object value.

For example:

Name (Form object name) = John Smith (Form object value)

If the user is asked to make a choice from an existing set of responses then you have to set both the name of the form object and its value from which the user can make a choice.

- **Text Fields**. There are three types of text field in Dreamweaver: Single-line, Multi-line and Password.

- **Hidden Fields**. You can enter information and script instructions for processing the form in a hidden field. The value of a hidden field is not visible to the user.

- **Text area**. Inserts a multi-line text field.

- **Checkboxes**. Enable users to make a selection (or multiple selections) by clicking in a box.

- **Radio Buttons**. Enable users to select one option from multiple choices. When you click on one radio button in a group any other selected button will automatically turn off.

When you are creating a form you may find it easier to align text with form objects if you work within a table. You should insert the form on the page first, then insert a table into the form and add your form objects and associated text to the table.

- **Lists/Menu**. Another way of offering users a selection of choices, lists and menus are useful in that they take up very little space on a page – particularly for very long lists such as countries. Lists differ from menus by allowing users to choose more than one selection and also enabling them to display more than one choice at a time on the page.

- **Jump Menu**. Use a list as a navigation tool (see the section in Chapter 4: Linking using jump menus).

- **Image Fields**. Add interest to your page by inserting an image to replace the standard grey submit button.

- **File Fields**. Inserts a Browse button and text field to allow users to attach and send files.

- **Buttons**. There are three types of form button – Submit, Reset and None. The Submit button sends the form to be processed by the script by using the link set up in the Form Action. The Reset button clears the form and resets its default values. The None button is used for other buttons used with scripts, such as a Go button with a search field.

Using form objects

Creating a single-line text field

1. Click on the **Text Field** button on the **Insert** bar.

2. The default text field that appears selected in the Property inspector will be Single-line (Figure 7.4).

3. In the **Property inspector** type in a field name in the textfield box, the number of characters (or width) of the field display and specify the maximum number of characters that a user can insert. Enter an initial value

if you want some text to appear in the text box when the form loads; for example, if you have asked for a name you could type an initial value, e.g. 'John Smith'.

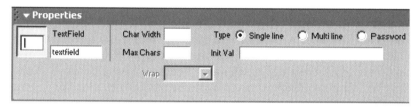

Figure 7.4 Text field properties.

Creating a multi-line text field

1. Insert a text field from the **Insert** bar and in the **Property inspector** select the **Type** option **Multi-line** or select the **Text area** button from the **Insert** bar.

2. Set the character width and set the number of lines to appear.

3. You can also set up word wrap options for a multi-line text field. Virtual will wrap the text when the user types to the edge of the box, but will *send* the data as a long character string, whereas Physical wrap will send the data wrapped as it appears on screen.

Inserting a password field

1. Insert a text field from the **Insert** bar and in the **Property inspector** select the **Password** option.

Your options in the Property inspector are the same as for a single-line text field.

Inserting checkboxes

Checkboxes give the user an easy-to-select option for making one or more selections from a group.

1. Click on the **Checkbox** button on the **Insert** bar.

2. In the **Property inspector** enter a name and a value for the checkbox (Figure 7.5). Each checkbox should have a different name and a value associated to it. For instance, you could be asking what sports the user enjoys. Each checkbox could have a different name such as 'Football' or 'Tennis' and the Checked Values of each of them could be set as 'True' or 'Yes'. This means that if the user has checked the Football box, the Checked Value of the box is True – the user enjoys football.

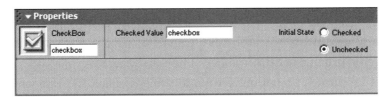

Figure 7.5 Checkbox properties.

3. Choose the **Initial State** of a checkbox as either 'checked' or 'unchecked'. This is used if you are assuming a positive response from the user and it is up to them to 'uncheck' the box. You often see this used when the question is asked, 'Do you want to receive promotional material from us in the future?' and the box is already checked!

Inserting radio buttons

Radio buttons are used when you want the user to select only one option from a group.

To insert radio buttons one at a time:

1. Click on the **Radio Button** in the **Insert** bar.
2. In the **Property inspector** (Figure 7.6) give the button a name and a value.

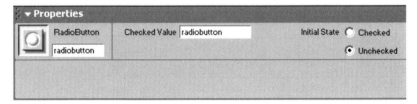

Figure 7.6 Radio button properties.

Unlike checkboxes it is essential that radio buttons all have the *same name* in order for them to work properly: that is turn 'On' and 'Off' in relation to each other. For example, if you want users to select their gender as male or female, both radio buttons would have the name 'Gender', and their values would be set as 'Male' and 'Female' respectively.

Inserting a radio button group

Rather than inserting radio buttons one at a time it is probably quicker to use the radio group button. It also avoids the risk of you misnaming a button that is part of a group. Once you have inserted a radio group you can always edit an individual button in the **Property inspector**.

1. Click on the **Radio group** button in the **Insert** bar.
2. In the **Radio Group** window (Figure 7.7) type in a name for the group.
3. Type in a label for each button and a value.
4. Click OK.

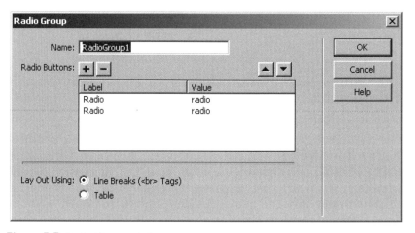

Figure 7.7 Radio Group window.

Adding a menu

Dreamweaver offers two different scrolling options: lists and menus. The main technical difference between them is that a menu is used to offer one selection from a group (like radio buttons) and a list enables the user to select more than one (like checkboxes).

1. Click on the **List/Menu** in the **Insert** bar.

2. In the **Property inspector** the default selection will be a **Menu** (Figure 7.8). Enter a name for the menu in the List/Menu box and click on the **List Values...** button.

3. In the **List Values** box (Figure 7.9) enter the item name that you wish to appear in the list and the value of that item – which is what will actually be sent back as data. For example, if you had a list of countries the name might be 'Australia' and the value 'Aus' – depending on how you intend to process the information.

4. You can add or delete items using the **(+)** and **(–)** buttons or change the order of appearance using the up and down arrows. Sadly there is no automatic way of getting your list in alphabetical order!

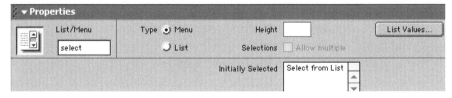

Figure 7.8 List/Menu properties.

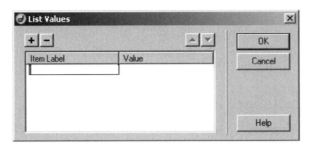

Figure 7.9 List Values window.

If you are using a scrolling list and wish users to be able to make multiple selections, give a thought to how they will do this – that is, will they know how? If you don't know, which many people don't, you hold down the **Ctrl/Cmd** key as you make the selections! It may be worthwhile adding a written instruction to the user.

Adding a list

1. Click on the **List/Menu** in the **Insert** bar.

2. In the **Property inspector** select the **List** option. Enter the name of the list and click on the **List Values...** button. Enter the names and values of your list items as you would with a menu (described above).

3. In the **Property inspector** you can choose the height of the list to make more options immediately visible, and you can also choose if you want to allow the user to make multiple selections. You can also set which list item you wish to make initially visible (scroll bars will allow users to view the other list items).

Inserting a file field

Use file fields to let users upload a file to their system.

1. Click on the **File Field** in the **Insert** bar.

2. In the **Property inspector**, name the field and enter the width of the field, and set the maximum characters allowed (Figure 7.10).

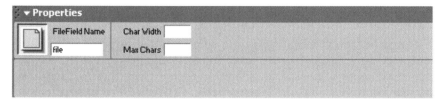

Figure 7.10 File field properties.

Adding a hidden field

1. Click on the **Hidden Field** button in the **Insert** bar.
2. Dreamweaver will insert an **Invisible Element** indicator in your file, which you can later select if you want to edit the field.
3. In the **Property inspector** (Figure 7.11) enter a unique field name and fill in the value box with the information you want to send with the form.

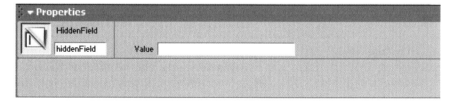

Figure 7.11 Hidden field properties.

When you are creating a drop-down list it's probably a good idea to make the top, visible selection something like 'Select from List'. Otherwise you won't know whether the user has actually selected the option at the top of the list or whether they simply haven't bothered to make a choice.

If you want users to send attached files with the form, check with your host server that anonymous file uploads are allowed.

Inserting form buttons

1. Click on the Button option in the **Insert** bar.

2. The **Submit** button will appear as the default selection in the **Property inspector** (Figure 7.12). You can leave the button labels as they are or you can change the button label to say something other than 'Submit', for example you may want your button label to appear as **Click here to send**.

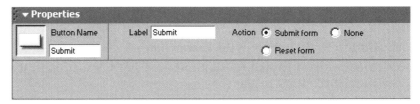

Figure 7.12 Form button properties.

3. For inserting **Reset** buttons or other buttons (None) follow the same process as above and make your selections in the **Property inspector**.

Inserting an image field

The image field offers you an alternative to using the usual grey Submit button. You need to have created a GIF in a graphics program and have it available in the site files to use it in a form.

1. Click on the **Image** button in the **Insert** bar.

2. In the **Property inspector** you can enter a name and value for the image field and other options as you would for other graphics on your site.

Some useful references

Some useful CGI resource sites to try are:

The CGI Resource Index: cgi.resourceindex.com

Matt's Script Archive: www.worldwidemart.com/scripts/

An excellent resource for explaining CGI and how to set one up can be found on Webmonkey –
http://www.hotwired.lycos.com/webmonkey/programming/perl_cgi/

Advanced formatting using styles

8

Understanding styles

Using HTML styles

Using Cascading Style Sheets (CSS)

Getting to know the style options

Creating a Custom Style (class)

Applying a Custom Style

Removing a Custom Style

Redefining an HTML tag

Using the CSS Selector

Editing styles

Creating an External Style Sheet

Linking a page to an External Style Sheet

Some useful references

Understanding styles

Dreamweaver enables you to create two types of formatting 'styles' – quite different in both their versatility and application. The first are HTML styles, which are simply a type of shortcut for applying text and paragraph formatting. For example, you could set up an HTML style that sets a font type to Verdana, colour to red and style to italics. The second type are Cascading Style Sheets, known as CSS, which offer far more advanced options for formatting and positioning page elements. Using CSS you can create styles to apply within a single Web page, or create a separate CSS file which defines various styles and can be linked to multiple pages in a site.

CSS are only recognised by browsers in version 4+, and even then, there are some differences between the way Microsoft Internet Explorer and Netscape Navigator handle style attributes. Older browsers will simply ignore them, leaving your carefully designed pages to the mercy of your viewers' default browser settings. It's a good idea to rigorously test styles across browsers and platforms (PC and Mac).

Using HTML styles

HTML styles enable you to define font type, colour, size or style (bold or italics) and to set paragraph alignment and formatting. You can then apply the style to selections of text or to whole paragraphs within a page.

To create an HTML style:

1. Go to the **Design** panel group and select the HTML styles tab (Figure 8.1).
2. Click on the **New Style** button at the bottom right of the panel to open the **Define HTML Style** window (Figure 8.2).

Figure 8.1 HTML Styles panel.

Or

In the **HTML Styles** panel, click on the menu indicator on the right and select **New**.

Or

Right/Ctrl-click on the **HTML Styles** panel and select **New**.

3. In the **Define HTML Style** dialog box, name the style in the **Name** box, choose whether the style will apply to a selection or a paragraph and select formatting options.

4. Click **OK** and the new style will appear in the **HTML Styles** panel under the two default style options.

Figure 8.2 HTML Styles option.

Applying an HTML style

1. Highlight some text or click in a paragraph.

2. From the **HTML Styles** panel check the box to the left of the Apply button to turn on the **Auto-apply** option.

3. Click on the style you wish to apply.

Removing an HTML style

1. Highlight some text or click in the paragraph from which you want to remove the style.
2. In the **HTML Styles** panel, click on either the **Clear Paragraph Style** or **Clear Selection Style** option.

Editing an HTML style

1. In the **HTML Styles** panel double-click on the style you wish to edit.
2. Edit the options and click **OK**.

Using Cascading Style Sheets (CSS)

You create CSS in two ways, either by redefining the attributes of a particular HTML tag, or by creating and naming a Custom style, which can be applied to any selection of text. Whichever type of style you use you can set it up within a page, where it will be available to that page *only*, or you can set it up externally, within a CSS file, and apply it to all or some of the pages within your site.

Getting to know the style options

1. To open the **CSS Styles** panel, go to the **Design** panel group and select the **CSS Styles** tab (Figure 8.3).
2. Click on the **New CSS Style** button along the bottom right of the panel to open the **New CSS Style** window (Figure 8.4).

   Or

   In the **CSS Styles** panel, click on the menu indicator on the right and select **New Style**.

When you edit an HTML style, Dreamweaver does not update or change any text to which you previously applied that style. The text is not linked to the style, as it would be with CSS.

Conflicting styles – if two or more styles are applied to the same text, the innermost style, for instance the tag nested closest to the text, will override the others – thus the sense of the name Cascading Style Sheets.

Figure 8.3 The CSS Styles panel.

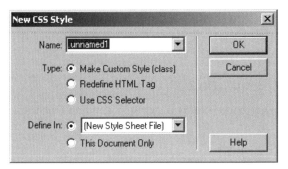

Figure 8.4 Selecting a CSS style.

Or

Right/Ctrl-click on the **CSS Styles** panel and select **New CSS Style**.

There are three CSS options available.

- **Make Custom Style (class)**. This is a type of style you can apply to a selection of text. You give the style a unique name, such as 'header' or 'bodytext', and then define its properties.
- **Redefine HTML Tag**. This style type enables you to redefine the formatting of a particular HTML tag. To use this option, you really need a fairly good knowledge of HTML tags and what they do. For instance, you may decide to redefine the heading tag <H1> so that every time the tag is used in a page it appears a certain size and colour.
- **Use CSS Selector**. The CSS Selector is used to define link properties available from the drop-down menu and also to format a particular combination of tags, for example if you typed TABLE H1 the style would apply to the <H1> tag only when used within a <TABLE> tag.

If the Custom Style is applied to a block of text, such as a paragraph, the CLASS attribute is applied to the particular tag which calls up the style, for example <P CLASS='header'>. If the Custom Style is applied to a word or sentence a <SPAN> tag, which contains the CLASS attribute, is inserted around it.

In the CSS Styles panel you can also choose to define the style either in a **New Style Sheet File** or in 'this document only'. Creating a New Style Sheet File, what is known as an External Style Sheet, will be covered later in this chapter.

To get started it's probably easiest if you choose to define the style in 'this document only' and, once you are familiar with styles and how they work, try creating an External Style Sheet.

Creating a Custom Style (class)

1. From the **New Style** dialog box, select the option **Make Custom Style (class)**.

2. Name the style in the Name box, which you will notice is preceded by a dot (Dreamweaver will automatically insert one if you delete it). Use only one word for style names (no spaces) and start the name with a letter rather than a number. The name can be anything that makes sense to you, for instance you may create Custom Styles for different heading types and therefore could call them 'heading1', 'heading2' and so on.

3. Select the radio button. **This document only**.

4. Click **OK** and the **Style definition** dialog box will appear (Figure 8.5).

5. Explore the different style attributes available. Click on the different categories on the left of the dialog box to explore the different style options.

6. Once you have chosen some options for your style, for instance a colour and a font size, click **OK** and your style will appear in the **CSS Styles** panel.

Applying a Custom Style

1. Select some text in your document, or place the cursor anywhere within a text paragraph (depending on how you wish to apply the style).

2. Check that the **Apply Styles** button is selected.

3. Click on the style in the **CSS Styles** panel.

You will see that the text changes immediately. Experiment with applying the style to text selections, paragraphs and specific tags. Remember you can easily select a tag by using the Tag Selector at the bottom of the document window.

*All of the different style options are too numerous to list here and are well described in the Dreamweaver O'Reilly Reference. You can look up any available style in the reference, which describes how the style works, any problems concerning the style and browser compatibility. To access the Reference go to the **Code** panel Group and click on the **Reference** tab. Choose O'Reilly CSS Reference from the **Book** drop-down menu.*

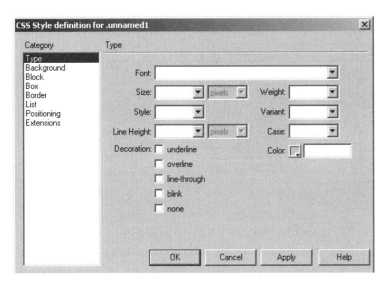

Figure 8.5 The CSS Styles definition window.

Removing a Custom Style

1. Select the text, paragraph or tag from which you want to remove the style.
2. From the **CSS Styles** panel select **None**.

Redefining an HTML tag

1. From the **New Style** dialog box, select the option **Redefine HTML** tag.
2. Select a **Tag** to redefine from the Tag drop-down menu (Figure 8.6).

There are some style attributes that will not display in the Dreamweaver document window and these are marked with an asterisk (*). These styles should be visible when you preview the page in a browser window. It is important to test your styles using both Microsoft Internet Explorer and Netscape Navigator as some styles appear differently in the browser windows, and some styles are not yet supported by either.

You can use the Property inspector to work with styles on a page by using the 'A' toggle to the left of the font drop-down menu.

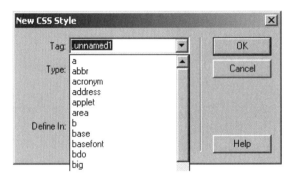

Figure 8.6 Redefining an HTML tag.

3. Click **OK** and the **Style definition** dialog box will appear.

4. Make your formatting selections and click **OK**.

The style will now apply any time you use that tag.

*You may have noticed on some Web pages that text links appear without underlining. Ever wondered how they do that? Simple ... it's done by redefining the link tag <A> and setting text-decoration to **None**!*

Using the CSS Selector

1. From the **New Style** dialog box, select the option **Use CSS Selector**.

2. Choose a selector from the drop-down menu which now appears at the top of the dialog box (the menu lists all the different link formatting options) or type into the Selector box a valid combination of tags (such as TABLE H2).

3. Click **OK** and the **Style definition** window will appear.

4. Make your formatting selections and click **OK**.

Editing styles

1. From the **CSS Styles** panel select the **Edit Styles** radio button.
2. Double-click on the style you want to edit.
3. Make your changes and click OK.

Creating an External Style Sheet

An External Style Sheet is a file that contains style definitions and is linked to pages in a Website. By having any of or all your pages linked to an External Style Sheet you can easily control style consistency throughout your site and easily make formatting changes across the site.

An External Style Sheet is actually a separate file, which resides in your site folder and has the extension '.css'.

To create an External Style Sheet:

1. From the **New Style** window, select the type of style you wish to define *within* the External Style Sheet.
2. Select the **Define In New Style Sheet** radio button.
3. The **Save Style Sheet File As...** window will appear. Browse to select where you want to save the file and name it – Dreamweaver will automatically add the '.css' extension.
4. Click **Save** and the **Style definition** window will open.
5. Make your style selections and click **OK**.

The page you are working in is now linked to the External Style Sheet. If you defined a Custom Style it will appear in the CSS Styles panel or if you redefined an HTML tag it will apply automatically in your page.

Be aware that the A:Hover option, which acts like a mouse rollover, works only in Microsoft Internet Explorer and Netscape 6.

*You can make your pages compatible with older browsers by converting your styles to HTML. To use the Dreamweaver convert option, go to **File > Convert > 3.0 Browser Compatible**.*

Be aware that once converted you may lose formatting in the process (because CSS offer so many options that HTML simply can't replicate) and you will no longer have the ability to make global changes to your pages.

Adding styles

To add styles to the External Style Sheet:

1. Select the **Edit Styles** radio button in the **CSS Styles** panel.
2. Highlight the CSS file name and select the **New CSS Style** button.
3. Choose which type of style you wish to add.
4. Make your selections in the **Style definition** window and click **OK**.

Linking a page to an External Style Sheet

1. From within the document you want to attach the style to, click on the **Attach Style Sheet** button in the CSS Styles panel.
2. Browse to select the .css file you want to link to.
3. Choose the **Add as Link** radio button as this method is supported by both Netscape Navigator and Microsoft Internet Explorer (Figure 8.7).
4. Click **OK** and the file will be attached.

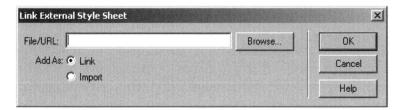

Figure 8.7 Link External Style window.

Some useful references

Get advice from THE experts at the World Wide Web Consortium. A huge reference resource.

http://www.w3.org/Style/CSS/

Let the HTML Writers Guild answer many of your CSS questions:

http://www.hwg.org/resources/faqs/cssFAQ.html

Advanced formatting using layers and timelines

9

Creating a layer

Putting content in a layer

Selecting a layer

Deleting a layer

Understanding layer properties

Working with layers

Changing layer preferences

Converting layers to tables

Animating layers with a timeline

Getting to know the timeline

Creating animation along a timeline

Dragging an animation path

Editing layers in the timeline

Modifying timelines

Adding behaviours to a timeline

Layers are floating boxes that can hold text, graphics and other page elements. Created using CSS positioning, layers enable you to position elements on a page by dragging them (which is a bit more like working in a graphics program) rather than struggling with HTML tables. You can place layers anywhere on a page, stack one on top of another, overlap portions of them and animate them using a timeline: what is known as Dynamic HTML (DHTML).

The major drawback of creating a page using layers is that they are only supported by browsers using version 4 and later and there are some discrepancies between Netscape Navigator and Microsoft Internet Explorer. Well, what's new?

If you are concerned with browser compatibility, you can convert layers into tables. This means that you can create a page using layers – to take advantage of the ease with which you can position elements – then convert to tables and ensure your Web page is 100% browser compatible!

The best way to get to grips with layers is to get stuck in – draw a couple of layers, insert some content and start moving them around a page!

Creating a layer

Before you begin working with layers open the **Layers** panel in the **Advanced Layout** panel group (Figure 9.1).

There are several different ways to create a layer:

- **Draw a layer**. Click the **Draw Layer** button in the **Layout** tab of the **Insert** bar and drag a layer in the document window (Figure 9.2).

  Or

- **Insert a layer**. Place your cursor where you want the layer to appear and choose **Insert > Layer**.

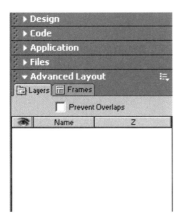

Figure 9.1 The Layers panel.

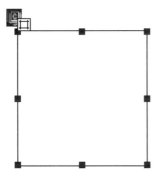

Figure 9.2 A layer, selection handle and Invisible Element icon.

*If you create a layer using the Insert option a layer will be displayed with default height and width attributes. You can change these attributes in your Preferences. Select **Edit > Preferences** and select **Layers** from the category list.*

*You can turn Invisible Elements on and off in the Preferences. Go to **Edit > Dreamweaver Preferences > Invisible Elements > Anchor Points for Layers**.*

Once you have created a layer an Invisible Element icon will appear on the page showing where the code is in the HTML. The Invisible Element icon appears only in the document window and not in the browser.

Putting content in a layer

1. Click inside a layer.
2. Type in text, insert an image or insert any other content as you would normally on a page. You can also drag objects into a layer.

Selecting a layer

To modify or move a layer you need to select it. When a layer is selected, eight black handles will appear around the layer.

To select a layer:

- Click the layer selection handle.
- Click on the **Invisible Element** icon in the document window.
- Click the border of the layer.
- Click on the layer in the **Layers** panel.

Deleting a layer

You can easily delete a layer by selecting it and clicking on the **Backspace** or **Delete** key.

Understanding layer properties

Select a layer to view formatting and positioning options in the Property inspector (Figure 9.3).

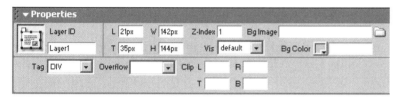

Figure 9.3 Layer properties.

- **Layer ID**. Name the layer to identify it for scripting (say for timelines or behaviours).

- **L and T**. Defines the position of a layer relative to the left (L) hand side of the page and the top (T) of the page. If your layer is nested in another layer the L and T will relate to the Left and Top of the parent layer. Try changing these values in the Property inspector to move your layer around the page or note how the values change as you drag a layer around the page.

- **W and H**. Displays the width and height of the layer. You can change the size of your layer by changing the values in the Property inspector or you can drag the resize handles. Width and height values will be overridden if you insert an object that exceeds the layer size – see *Overflow*.

- **Z-index**. Controls the visibility of overlapping layers, also known as the stacking order. A layer with a higher Z-index will appear above a layer with a lower number. You can change the stacking order of layers by typing in a different number (higher or lower) in the Z-index window.

- **Bg Image**. You can select a background image for your layer just as you would for a page.

- **Bgcolor**. Set the background colour of a layer just as you would for a page, a table or a table cell.

- **Vis**. Determines the visibility of the layer when the page loads. You can also change layer visibility to turn layers On and Off dynamically along a time-line – see Editing layers in the timeline later in this chapter. Vis options are:

  Visible – Displays the layer regardless of the parent properties.

  Hidden – Hides the layer regardless of the parent properties.

  Inherit – Forces the layer to inherit the properties of the parent element.

  Default – Usually visible unless a layer is nested, in which case it will inherit the value of the parent layer.

- **Tag**. Select your layer as a CSS layer (SPAN and DIV) or a Netscape layer (LAYER and ILAYER). It is recommended that you use the DIV or SPAN tags as they are supported by both Netscape Navigator and Microsoft Internet Explorer versions 4+, whereas the LAYER and ILAYER tags are supported only by Netscape.

- **Overflow**. Determines what happens to content larger than the layer dimensions. Overflow options are:

  Visible – Shows overflow content.

  Hidden – Hides overflow content.

  Scroll – Provides scroll bars to view overflow content.

  Auto – Provides scrollbars where needed to view overflowing content.

- **Clip**. Different from overflow as it defines the visible content of the actual layer and has no relation to content outside the dimensions of the layer such as overflow. The options are T (top), R (right), B (bottom) and L (left). A value attributed to one of these options is not related to the page but to the

Make sure you test across platforms and browsers if you use overflow options as they are not well supported by Netscape Navigator (though they are OK in Version 6) nor by Micro-soft Internet Explorer on the Mac.

edges of the layer. For example, your layer could have a dimension of 300 ¥ 100 pixels and you could define the clipping area as L = 150, cutting the visible width of the layer in half (R=150 would also halve the layer visibility but would clip from the other side).

Working with layers

Moving layers
Click on the layer selection handle and drag the layer to reposition. For precise layer positioning either:

■ Use the arrow keys with a selected layer to move it one pixel at a time.

Or

■ Change the **L** and **T** values of a layer in the **Property inspector**.

Positioning and aligning layers
For layer positioning you may find it useful to use the **Grid** and **Snap to Grid** function.

■ To turn on the grid go to **View > Grid > Show Grid**.

■ To change the grid settings go to **View > Grid > Edit Grid** (Figure 9.4).

■ To snap layers to the grid go to **View > Grid > Snap To**.

To align more than one layer at a time, select the layers (hold down the shift key to make multiple selections) and make the positioning changes in the Property inspector. Note that you can use this option to make other changes to multiple layers.

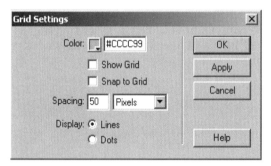

Figure 9.4 Grid Settings.

Nesting layers

A nested layer is one that sits inside another layer (Figure 9.5).

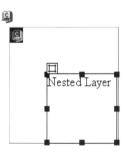

Figure 9.5 A nested layer.

There are several different ways to create a nested layer. You can:

- Place your cursor in a layer and choose **Insert > Layer**.

  Or

- Click on the **Draw Layer** button in the **Layout** or **Common** tab of the **Insert** bar then place your cursor in a layer and draw the new, nested layer.

Once you have created a nested layer, look in the Layers panel and you'll see that it appears indented beneath the parent layer.

You can also create a nested layer from the Layers panel. To do so:

- Hold down the Ctrl/Cmd key and drag a layer in the Layers panel over the proposed parent layer. When you release the mouse the layer should appear indented beneath the parent layer.

The easiest way to 'unnest' a layer is by using the Layers panel:

- Select the nested layer and drag the layer away from the parent layer.

Overlapping layers

The ability to overlap layers is one of their most useful and versatile design functions.

To overlap layers (but not nest them) simply drag one layer over another. If you are unable to do this, confirm that the **Prevent Overlaps** box in the Layers panel is not checked.

If you can't seem to nest a layer the option may be turned off in the Dreamweaver Preferences. To turn them on go to **Edit > Preferences > select** *the category* **Layers** *and check the* **Nesting** *checkbox.*

If you plan to work in layers and then convert to tables make sure you have the **Prevent Overlaps** *box checked as Dreamweaver can't convert overlapping layers into tables.*

Changing the stacking order of layers

The stacking order or Z-index of layers determines how overlapping layers will appear – those with a higher number appear on top.

To change the stacking order of layers you can change the Z-index number either in the Property inspector or in the Layers panel, but it is probably easier and less confusing if you simply drag layers above or below each other in the Layers panel.

Changing layer visibility

You can hide or show layers either by changing the visibility setting in the Property inspector or by clicking in the column underneath the eye icon in the Layers panel.

Changing layer preferences

Set your layer preferences to determine the settings for new layers that you insert (Figure 9.6). To access Layer Preferences go to **Edit > Preferences** and click on the **Layers** category.

The available preferences are:

- Tag
- Visibility
- Width and height
- Background colour
- Background image.

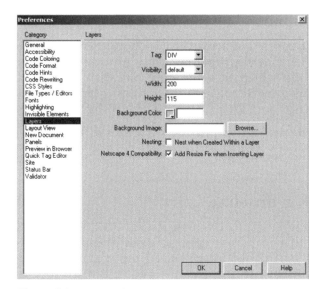

Figure 9.6 Layer preferences.

All of the preferences are explained in the Understanding layer properties section earlier in this chapter.

The two other options available are:

1. Nest when created within a layer, which is explained in the section Working with layers.

2. Netscape 4 compatibility – make sure this is checked to ensure layers are positioned properly in Netscape 4.

Converting layers to tables

To ensure that your pages are consistent across browsers you may choose to convert your layers to tables. You may also find that you like to switch between working in layers and tables in which case you may also wish to convert between tables and layers. Dreamweaver makes either process very simple. To convert layers to tables:

Go to **File > Convert > 3.0 Browser Compatible > Layers to Table**.

When you have made a selection you will see that Dreamweaver has created a new page for the new format.

Animating layers with a timeline

Timelines are used to animate layers using Dynamic HTML (DHTML). Layers in a timeline can be animated to move across a page, become visible and invisible and change stacking order. You can also attach behaviours to a timeline (see Chapter 10: Working with behaviours).

Getting to know the timeline

To open the timeline:

Go to **Window > Others > Timelines** (Figure 9.7).

Elements of the timeline are:

- **Timeline name**. Displays the name of the current timeline and allows you to choose other timelines from the drop-down menu.
- **Rewind button**. Takes you back to the beginning of the timeline.

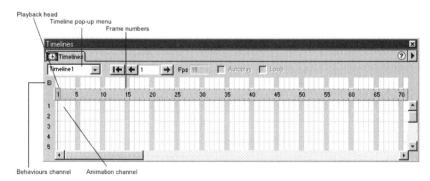

Figure 9.7 The timeline.

- **Back and forward buttons**. Take you back or forward one frame. If you hold down the mouse the timeline will play backwards or forwards. The window between the buttons displays the current frame number.

- **Fps**. The animation playback rate of frames per second. The default setting is 15fps, which is a good average rate across systems.

- **Autoplay**. Check this if you want the animation to play automatically when the page downloads.

- **Loop**. Check this if you want the animation to loop continually when the page has downloaded. To set a specific number of loops see the Behaviour example at the end of this chapter.

- **Behaviours channel**. Behaviours can be added to the timeline, for example to show or hide layers, or to jump to a particular frame in a timeline.

When you have added a behaviour a marker will appear in the Behaviors channel which you can then click on to edit the behaviour.

- **Frame numbers and the playback head**. Indicates the frame numbers. The playback head shows which frame of the animation is currently being displayed in the document window.

- **Animation Bar**. Displays the frames relating to a layer in the timeline.

- **Keyframe**. Frames that appear with an embedded circle indicate a frame with a specific attribute, such as the position or visibility of a layer.

- **Animation Channels**. Displays the animation bars for each separate layer.

Creating animation along a timeline

The first thing you need to do to create an animation is to add a layer to the timeline. Make sure you have the timeline open.

1. Select the layer you wish to animate.

2. Drag the layer on to the animation bar in the **Timeline**.

   Or

   From the main window go to **Modify > Timeline > Add Object to Timeline**.

Once you have added a layer to the timeline it will appear in the first channel of the timeline. To animate a timeline you set up beginning and end points of the animation using what are known as keyframes. The keyframes are the essence of animating between two or more points.

To animate the layer:

1. Click on the first keyframe in the layer animation bar.
2. Position your layer from where you want it to begin to animate.
3. Click on the last keyframe in the layer animation bar.
4. Position the layer where you want it to be at the end of the sequence.
5. Hold down the forward button along the top of the timeline to see how the animation looks.

If you want the layer to move along a curve you need to insert a new keyframe. You can do this in several ways:

1. **Ctrl/Cmd**-click on a frame in the animation bar somewhere between the beginning and end keyframes.
2. Select **Add key frame**.
3. Move your layer to a new position on the page and the animation will create a curve between the three keyframes.

Dragging an animation path

You can drag a path for your animation if it is simpler than creating multiple keyframes.

1. Select the layer and position it where you want the animation to begin.
2. From the main window go to **Modify > Timeline > Record Path of Layer**.
3. Drag the layer where you wish the animation to go.
4. Release where you want the animation to end.
5. Preview the animation by holding down the forward button.

Images that are in hidden layers are still downloaded with the page so are available to use when you change the layer visibility.

Editing layers in the timeline

You can use timelines to alter other properties of your layers, not simply positioning. For instance you can use a keyframe to reset the layer visibility, size and stacking order.

To edit layer properties on the timeline:

1. Add a layer to the **Timeline**.
2. Select or insert a **Keyframe**.
3. Change the layer properties in the **Property inspector**.
4. Preview the changes by holding down the forward button.

Once you have changed layer properties, for instance if you have set visibility to **Hidden**, that property will remain until the timeline hits the next keyframe where the visibility may, for example, be set back to **Visible**.

Modifying timelines

You can change the length of an animation, the position of the keyframes, the frame where the animation begins and so on. Practise moving frames and repositioning whole animation sequences on a timeline to see how different layers animate best.

To modify a timeline you can access the Timeline Edit menu in several ways:

- Choose **Modify > Timeline** *or*
- **Right/Ctrl**-click on a frame *or*
- Click on the top right arrow in the **Timelines** inspector.

Some useful editing options are:

- To make an animation longer add frames by dragging the end frame to extend the animation bar. You will notice that all the other keyframes move to maintain their relative positions in the animation.

- If you want to move an entire animation sequence on your page, select the animation bar in the Timelines inspector then drag the sequence on the page to the new position.

- To change where on the timeline a particular animation sequence starts, select the entire animation bar and drag it to a new frame position.

- You can copy and paste timeline sequences either within the same timeline but at another frame position, or in another timeline selected from the drop-down menu.

Adding behaviours to a timeline

You can add behaviours to timelines to trigger events when the timeline reaches a particular frame. For example, you can change the visibility of a layer or prompt a new timeline to play.

If you haven't used behaviours before you might find it useful to refer to Chapter 10: Working with behaviours before attempting to add behaviours to a timeline.

To add a behaviour to a timeline:

1. Click in the **Behaviors** channel at the frame position where you want the behaviour to occur. (If you double-click, the Behaviors panel will open.)

*Hold down the **Ctrl/Cmd** key while dragging the end frame to stop other frames from moving.*

If you copy and paste an animation sequence into a document that doesn't have a layer of that name, Dreamweaver copies the layer and the sequence from the original page.

If your page involves quite complex animation sequences, try creating multiple timelines and using them to control different parts of your page. Access the timeline drop-down menu (Right/ctrl-click on a timeline) and select **Add Timeline**. *You can then access your different time-lines by clicking on the drop-down arrow next to the Timeline name.*

2. Click on the plus (**+**) button and select a behaviour.

3. Fill in the dialog box associated with that behaviour.

4. Click **OK** and test your behaviour in the browser.

Behaviour example

A useful behaviour is to set a specific number of times for the page to loop after downloading.

1. Check the **Autoplay** option in the timeline and on the **Loop** option.

2. Click on the marker that will have appeared in the Behavior channel in the Timeline inspector. This will open up the Behaviors panel.

3. In the **Behaviors** panel double-click on the action **Go To Timeline Frame** (that is, click on the actual words).

4. In the Go To Timeline Frame window (Figure 9.8), type the number of times you want the animation to loop in the **Loop** field.

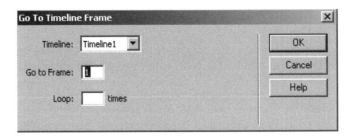

Figure 9.8 Go To Timeline Frame window.

Working with behaviours

Attaching a behaviour to an object

Editing a behaviour

Deleting a behaviour

Some common behaviours

Adding behaviours to Dreamweaver

Behaviours are used to enhance page functionality and user interactivity. Probably the best-known behaviour is a mouse rollover, where the user moves the cursor over an image (often a button) and the image is swapped for another. Behaviours are created using JavaScript, and there are many different ways to use them, for instance you can detect if a required form field has been filled in, or detect the user's browser version and send them to an appropriate page. As was mentioned in Chapter 9, behaviours can also be used to control a timeline.

Adding behaviours to your page using Dreamweaver is fairly straightforward but an understanding of the basic JavaScript concepts should help you understand how the behaviours work and help you to import JavaScript that's not included as an option in Dreamweaver.

JavaScript works using objects, events and actions.

- **Objects** are HTML elements such as images or the HTML page.
- **Events** are when something happens to an object, for instance the user quits a page. Some common events are *onMouseOver*, for when the user moves the mouse over an object, *onClick* for when they click on an object or *onLoad* for when the page downloads.
- **Actions** are what happen when an event occurs with an object, for example, the user has moved the mouse over (event) an image (object) and the image changes (action).

Attaching a behaviour to an object

To get started with behaviours you need to open the Behaviors panel (Figure 10.1). To do so:

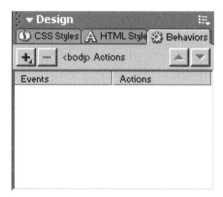

Figure 10.1 The Behaviors panel.

1. Go to **Window > Behaviors** or select the **Behaviors** tab in the **Design** panel group.

   In the Behaviors panel you have an Events column and an Actions column. You access the actions available for that object using the **plus (+)** button at the top left of the panel. The options will be different depending on the object. Once you have selected an action you will also have the option of changing the event associated with it.

2. Select an object (such as an image). If you want to add a behaviour to the whole page select the **<BODY>** tag using the tag selector at the bottom of the document window.

3. In the Behaviors panel click on the (+) button to access the drop-down menu of available actions (Figure 10.2).

*Text has to be a link for you to be able to attach a behaviour to it. If you want to create a dummy link, highlight the text and type a hash **(#)** key into the **Link** box in the **Property inspector**.*

Figure 10.2 Behavior actions.

Be aware that the user may find a dummy link confusing and try to click on a link that doesn't exist!

4. Fill in the associated dialog box to define the details of the behaviour. The box will be different for each action.

5. Dreamweaver will automatically select an event (such as onClick) to go with the action. To change the event, click on the arrow in the Behaviors panel and select a new event (Figure 10.3).

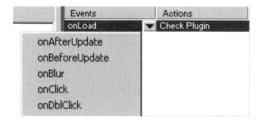

Figure 10.3 Example of available events.

Editing a behaviour

You may wish to change the action associated with an object or change the event that will trigger the action.

To edit an action:

1. Select the object that has the behaviour attached to it.
2. Double-click on the action in the Behaviors panel.
3. Make your changes in the associated dialog box and click **OK**.

Attaching an additional action

You can add more than one action to a particular event, for instance when a user rolls the mouse over an image, the image might change and some text appear in the browser Status bar.

1. Select the object that has a behaviour attached to it.
2. Click on the **plus (+)** sign and select a new action.

*The events available for different behaviours will change according to which browser version you are targeting. To see which events are associated with which browser version, in the Behaviors panel click on the arrow in the **Events** column and choose **Show Events For** (Figure 10.4). Note that the arrow will be available only if you have already applied a behaviour.*

Changing the order of actions to be called

Actions that are higher in the Behaviors panel will be the first to be called when the event occurs. To change the order of actions:

1. Select the action you wish to move in the **Behaviors** panel.
2. Click on the up and down arrows at the top of the Behaviors panel.

Changing the event associated with an action

1. Highlight the action in the **Behaviors** panel.
2. Click on the arrow in the **Events** column and select a new event.

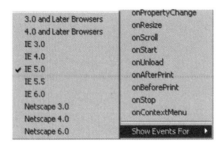

Figure 10.4 Select which browsers to show events for.

Deleting a behaviour

1. Select the object that has the attached behaviour.
2. In the **Behaviors** panel click on the behaviour you want to delete.
3. Click on the **minus (–)** button.

Some common behaviours

This is a brief overview of some of the more commonly used behaviours that are included in Dreamweaver (see Figure 10.2). Remember that these are only a selection of common JavaScripts. You can find many other scripts on the Web, and you can also add scripts to Dreamweaver using the Extension Manager, which is described at the end of this chapter.

- **Check Browser**. Used to check the browser that the visitor is using and then direct them to a certain page accordingly. For instance, if you have set up a particular CSS style that works only in a certain browser you may send your visitors who are not using that browser to a page that doesn't use the CSS.
- **Check Plugin**. Checks to see if a user has a certain plugin and directs them to one of two pages – one for **Found** that requires the plugin and another for **Otherwise** if the plugin is not found.
- **Go To URL**. Allows you to open a URL in a page or frame. It is most commonly used in a frames structure to open up more than one page in different frames. (As you know with ordinary HTML links you can open up only one new page from a link.)
- **Jump Menu**. This option allows you to edit an existing jump menu by double-clicking on the jump menu in the Behaviors panel (see the section in Chapter 4: Linking using jump menus).
- **Jump Menu Go**. Allows you to add a Go button to an existing jump menu.
- **Open Browser Window**. By using this behaviour rather than an HTML link to open a new browser window you can control how you want that new window to be displayed. For example, you can set the size of the window and whether you want navigation and menu bars to appear.

- **Play Sound**. Use this option to play sound when a page loads or when a certain event occurs, for example if the user rolls the mouse over an object.

- **Popup Message**. Displays a popup or 'alert' message to the user when triggered by an action.

- **Preload Images**. This preloads images that do not appear when the page first loads in the browser, for example, images to be called up with a mouse rollover. Notice that if you set up a rollover from the **Insert** bar the **Preload Images** behaviour will be added by default.

- **Set Text of Status Bar**. Is fairly self-explanatory and sets the text to appear at the bottom of the browser window, known as the Status bar.

- **Show/Hide Layers**. Used to hide or display layers when the user clicks on a link or rolls over an object. For this behaviour to work a layer must already be set up on the page and the behaviour should be attached to the *object that triggers* the action, such as a link, not to the layer being hidden/shown.

- **Swap Image**. This action swaps one image for another and is typically used with the mouse rollover event. Images being swapped must have the same dimensions, otherwise the second image to appear will be expanded or contracted to fit the dimensions of the original image.

- **Swap Image Restore**. Used with a mouse rollover to change the second (rollover) image back to the original when the user moves the mouse away.

- **Timeline**. There are three options available for timeline behaviours:

  1. *Go To Timeline Frame* – You can use an event to trigger the timeline to go to a specific frame.

  2. *Play Timeline* – This action is placed in the <BODY> tag when you have selected Autoplay with your timeline. You can also use it to play a timeline when an event occurs.

3. *Stop Timeline* – Stops the timeline when an event occurs.

■ **Validate Form**. Allows you to make certain fields, or textboxes, 'required' in a form. When a user doesn't fill them in properly they will get an alert message when they try to submit the form.

Adding behaviours to Dreamweaver

Dreamweaver comes installed with an Extension Manager (Figure 10.5), which allows you to download new features for Dreamweaver known as extensions. Downloading extensions can be really useful as there are new scripts being written all the time and most are available to download free of charge.

To validate individual fields as a user is filling them in, select the actual field and add the behaviour to it. To validate a form when the user clicks the Submit button, select the **<FORM>** *tag and attach the behaviour to it.*

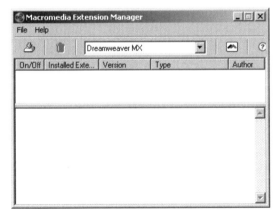

Figure 10.5 The Extension Manager.

To open the **Extension Manager** go to **Help > Manage Extensions**.

The best resource to download from is the Macromedia Exchange (www.macro-media.com/exchange/dreamweaver). To download extensions:

1. Click on the download option for the extension you wish to add.

2. Find the icon of the extension (.mxp) and double-click on it, which lets the Extension Manager install it for you.

3. You will probably have to restart Dreamweaver and you will see that the behaviour is now available as an action in your Behaviors panel.

Templates, libraries and other assets

11

Creating templates
Creating editable regions in a template
Creating new pages from a template
Attaching existing pages to a template
Detaching pages from a template
Changing template preferences
Creating library items
Inserting a library item
Editing a library item
Detaching objects from a library
Using the Assets panel
Using Assets from the site list
Adding assets to the Favorites list
Removing assets from the Favorites list
Creating a Favorites folder

Templates and libraries are Dreamweaver features that can help you to create and maintain pages efficiently and control consistency throughout your site.

Templates create a page blueprint from which other pages can be created. This not only allows you to create new pages quickly but also enables you to change multiple pages attached to a template. Templates are also useful for protecting pages (particularly those edited by multiple users) by allowing you to divide a page into editable and non-editable blocked regions.

Library items contain page elements that appear many times throughout your site, such as an email address, a copyright statement or even a set of navigation buttons. Library items can contain text, images, links, scripts and just about any elements you use on a page.

Both library items and templates are displayed as part of the Assets panel. From the Assets panel you can also create colour palettes for the site and manage other site 'asset' files such as images and URLs.

Creating templates

There are several ways to create a template in Dreamweaver. You may have already designed a page and want to convert it into a template for other pages, or you may want to create a template from scratch.

Before you start working with **Templates** select the **Template** tab on the **Insert** bar (Figure 11.1). Also open the **Templates** panel which is displayed in the **Assets** panel. To access it go to **Window > Assets** and select the **Templates** button on the left (Figure 11.2).

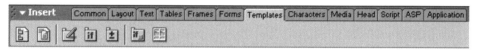

Figure 11.1 Template options on the Insert bar.

Figure 11.2 The Templates section of the **Assets** panel.

When you create and save a template Dreamweaver automatically creates a Template folder in your site files. Templates are stored in this folder and are given the extension '.dwt' (Dreamweaver template).

To create a new blank template:

1. Go to File > New to open the New Document window.
2. Select Template page and make sure the type is HTML Template.
3. Click the create button.

To convert a page to a template:

1. With the page open, Go to File > Save as Template.

Or

With the page open click the Make Template button in the Insert bar.

2. Name the template in the Save as Template window (Figure 11.3).

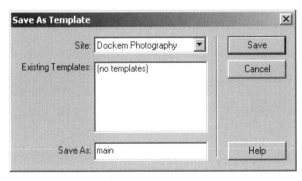

Figure 11.3 Save as Template window.

Creating editable regions in a template

When you create a template in Dreamweaver, all areas of the page are locked or non-editable by default. You need to specify which areas you want to be able to change in pages created from the template by identifying them as editable regions.

You can create editable areas in a template by either selecting existing content, or placing the cursor where you want the editable region to begin.

To mark content as editable:

1. Open the template by double-clicking on the **Template** icon in the Templates panel.

   Or

   Click on the template name and select the **Edit** icon on the bottom of the panel.
2. Select the page content you want to make editable.
3. In the **Insert** bar, select the **Editable Region** button.
4. In the dialog box name the editable region (Figure 11.4).

You can identify a place on the page that you would like to make editable – that is, where there is no existing content in the template. To create an editable region:

1. Open the template.
2. Place your cursor on the page where you want to insert the editable region.
3. In the **Insert** bar, select the **Editable Region** button.
4. In the dialog box name the editable region.

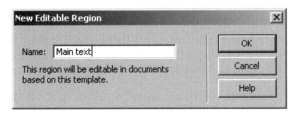

Figure 11.4 Naming an editable region.

Creating new pages from a template

There are several different ways to create a new page from a template:

When you add content to a page created from a template, you will find that you can only type into areas marked as editable. For editable regions that have no content in the template you should highlight the region name and insert your page content as normal.

1. Go to the **Templates** panel.
2. Select a template.
3. Right/Ctrl-click and select **New** from Template from the context menu.
   Or
   Open a new page and drag a template from the **Templates** panel on to it.
   Or
   Open a new page and go to **Modify > Templates >Apply Template to Page**.

Attaching existing pages to a template

Open an existing page and:

1. Go to **Modify > Templates >Apply Template to Page**.
2. Select a template.

Or

Drag a template from the **Templates** panel on to the page.

Or

Choose a template in the **Templates** panel and click on the **Apply** button.

Detaching pages from a template

If you want to make changes to a page that is attached to a template and the area is not an editable region you first need to detach it. Remember that once you have detached a page from a template it will no longer reflect any later edits made to that template.

1. Open the page to detach.

2. Go to **Modify > Templates > Detach from Template**.

Changing template preferences

As you have seen when you have created a page from a template, Dreamweaver identifies editable and locked areas with blocks of colour. To change the default colours:

1. Go to **Edit > Preferences**.

2. Select **Highlighting** in the category list.

3. Change colours and click **OK**.

Creating library items

Library items are useful for inserting page elements that you use repeatedly and which may be updated frequently. Once you have created a library item you can simply drag it into any page and each instance of that item will be linked to the library.

To create a library item:

When you create a library item in Dreamweaver it automatically creates a Library folder in the local root folder. Library items are stored in this folder and can be identified by the .lbi (library item) suffix.

1. Open the **Library** panel, which, like Templates, is part of the **Assets** panel.
2. Select the object you want to add to the library.
3. Drag the object into the blank window in the **Library** panel.
   Or
   Select the **New Library Item** icon on the bottom of the Library panel.
   Or
   Go to **Modify > Library > Add Object to Library**.
4. Name the new library item (Figure 11.5).

Inserting a library item

To insert a library item on a page:

1. Place the cursor where you want the item to appear.
2. Highlight the item name in the **Library** panel and click the **Insert** button.
   Or
   From the **Library** panel drag the library item on to the page.

Figure 11.5 Naming a library item.

Editing a library item

To edit a library item:

1. Double-click on the item in the **Library** panel.

   Or

   Highlight the item in the **Library** panel and select the **Edit** button at the bottom of the Library panel.

2. Make your changes to the library item and then close the window.

3. A dialog box will appear to ask if you want to update all the pages in your site that include the library item, so select '**Yes**'.

If you want to edit a library item but not immediately update all the related pages:

1. Make your changes to the library item and then close the window.

2. In the dialog box select 'No' to the update documents option.

3. When you are ready to update pages go to ***Modify > Library > Update Pages***.

Detaching objects from a library

If you want to change a particular instance of a library item without changing other instances of that item you need to detach it from the original. To do so:

1. Select the library item in the page where you want to edit it.

2. In the **Property inspector** click on the **Detach from Original** button (Figure 11.6).

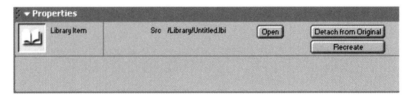

Figure 11.6 Library item properties.

Remember that once an item is detached from the original library item the link between them is effectively broken and it will no longer reflect changes made to the original library item.

Using the Assets panel

The Assets panel is where you manage templates and library items as well as other site assets such as images, Flash movies and colours. Assets are divided into two categories – one is the site category, which displays all of the assets used in the site, and the other is the favourites category, to which you can add favourite assets such as links to other Websites or colours.

To open the Assets panel go to **Window > Assets** (Figure 11.7).

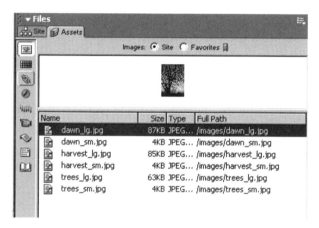

Figure 11.7 The Assets panel.

Using Assets from the site list

1. Position your cursor where you want the asset to be inserted, for instance an image, or highlight the text to which you want to apply an asset, for instance to make a link.
2. In the **Assets** panel select the asset you want to use.
3. Drag the asset on to the document window.
   Or
   Click on the **Insert** button in the **Assets** panel.

*As you work in your site, assets will only be added to the Assets panel when the site has either been closed and then re-opened, or you click on the **Refresh Site List** button at the bottom of the Assets panel.*

Adding assets to the Favorites list

The Favorites list can be useful when you are working on a large site with lots of assets. You can easily access assets that you can commonly use, and you can also group related favourites in folders.

To add an asset to the Favorites list:

1. Select the asset in the site list.
2. Click on the **Add to Favorites** button at the bottom of the Assets panel.

   Or

1. Select the asset in the document window, for instance an image.
2. Right/Ctrl-click and select **Add to Image Favorites** (if it is an image).

Removing assets from the Favorites list

1. Select the asset in the Favorites list.
2. Click on the **Remove from Favorites** at the bottom of the Assets panel.

Creating a Favorites folder

1. Click on the **New Favorites Folder** button at the bottom of the Assets panel.
2. Give the folder a name.
3. Drag related assets into the folder.

Getting dynamic with databases

What you need to get started

Setting up Dreamweaver MX

Setting up a Testing Server

Setting up the database

Creating a DSN

Connecting to your database

Entering data fields in a page

Updating your database

Adding a record

Deleting a record

Some useful references

12

Being able to create database-generated Web pages is the major feature of Dreamweaver MX that sets it apart from previous Dreamweaver versions. You may already be familiar with another Macromedia product, Ultradev, which used the Dreamweaver interface but had the added capacity to allow database integration. Well Ultradev and Dreamweaver have now basically been integrated and further developed in Dreamweaver MX so you can do it all in the one program.

In terms of process, working with database-driven sites is similar to working with a static site in that the site and the database are created and tested locally and once you are ready to go live, both the site and the database are uploaded to the server. Have a look at the process outlined in Figure 12.1. You may notice that it's a bit different than the process of creating static HTML pages described in Chapter 1, in that the server has to request content from the database, put it into the relevant HTML page and then send it on. Once your database is uploaded you can then edit it – add new entries, delete old ones, all from within the Dreamweaver MX interface.

Sound a bit daunting? Well, it does take a bit of setting up and testing, but when you've done it once you'll find it fairly straightforward to develop your skills further.

In this chapter we are going to cover what you need to create a basic database-driven Web page. As a sample, we'll create a 'What's On' page for our fictitious gallery site. We will go through how to extract and display the 'What's On' events stored in the database, and also how to add and delete events.

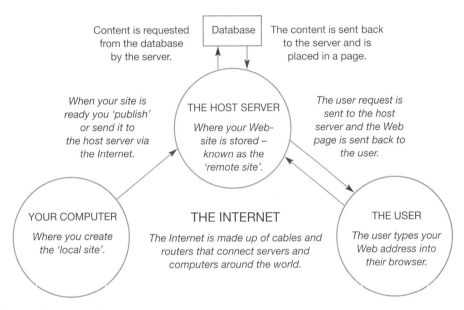

Content is requested from the database by the server.

Database

The content is sent back to the server and is placed in a page.

THE HOST SERVER

Where your Web-site is stored – known as the 'remote site'.

When your site is ready you 'publish' or send it to the host server via the Internet.

The user request is sent to the host server and the Web page is sent back to the user.

YOUR COMPUTER

Where you create the 'local site'.

THE INTERNET

The Internet is made up of cables and routers that connect servers and computers around the world.

THE USER

The user types your Web address into their browser.

Figure 12.1 How the server works.

What you need to get started

With Dreamweaver MX you can set up your system to work with various server technologies such as ASP or Coldfusion on different servers. There are enough options to suit anyone's system, but for reasons of space and simplicity we are going to use an Access database on a Windows server running **ASP** (Active Server Pages) – which are also fairly common systems that a lot of people use.

Pages created using ASP will have the extension .asp, not .html.

The three main elements of working with a database in Dreamweaver MX are:

1. **A Web server:** This is a piece of software that you need to run on your system in order to process database Web pages. On Windows the server software comes free – either Internet Information Server (IIS) or Personal Web Server (PWS). The software may or may not be already installed so the first thing you need to do is to check whether it is.

   From the Windows Finder look at your folders and see if there is a C:/Inetpub or D:/Inetpub folder. If you can't locate the folders you probably need to install a server. See Appendix C – Setting up and testing a Web server.

2. **A database:** A database is used to store information on your computer using a tabular format. If you are a total beginner and have never used a database it is worth getting to grips with setting one up and extracting data before attempting to use one with Dreamweaver MX. Access is a database that comes as part of the Microsoft Office suite and is easy to use. It is also the database that we will be using in this chapter for examples. To know more about using Access databases see the end of this chapter for some references and tutorials.

3. **A connection to the database:** This allows the Web server application to talk to your database using a driver such as ODBC (Open Database Connectivity) which also comes with Windows. One of the simplest connections to set up, and the one we will be explaining here, is a system DSN (Data Source Name).

Setting up Dreamweaver MX

To create a dynamic Website using Dreamweaver you need to set up a **local** site. One option for managing all of your dynamic sites is to store them under C:\Inetpub\wwwroot. Make sure that your site is in its own folder (or directory), for example C:\Inetpub\wwwroot\dockem, so that you can then continue to create different folders in the wwwroot for your different sites.

Setting up a testing server

1. Open the **Site Definition** window by going to **Window > Edit Sites** and select your site.

2. Select the **Advanced** tab at the top of the window.

3. Select **Testing Server** from the category list (Figure 12.2).

4. Select the Server Model as **ASP VBScript**.

5. Browse to and select the Testing Server folder.

6. Set the URL Prefix to 'http://localhost/your_site_name

Setting up the database

Using Microsoft Access you need to set up a database from which information can be extracted. As an example we will set up a 'What's On' page for the photographic gallery in a one-table database called 'Events' with four fields:

1. An ID field which provides a unique identifier for each of the database records (set to Auto/number). This should also be set as your primary key.

2. A field for the date of each event (set to Date/Time).

Once you understand the set-up procedures and if you are building your site from scratch you may find it easiest to do all of your site set-up using the set-up wizard. Go to **Site > New >** *and click on the Basic Tab to work through the options.*

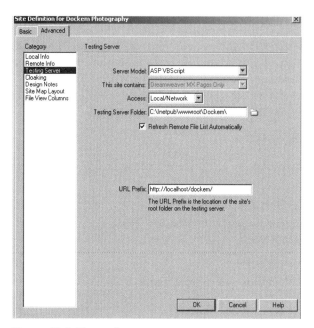

When you are naming a date field in Access, use something like 'event_date' rather than simply 'date', as the word 'date' is used in scripting and can cause computer confusion. It actually makes life easier to precede all of your field names with the name of the table.

Figure 12.2 Testing Server set-up options.

3. A field describing where the event is (set to Text field – which can go up to 255 characters).

4. A field describing the event (set to Memo – which can be more than 255 characters).

Creating a DSN

To set up your DSN the first thing you should do is make sure you have the latest version of **MDAC** (Microsoft Data Access Components) running (at the moment, version 2.7). To download go to: www.microsoft.com/data/download.htm

To set up a DSN:

1. Locate the System DSN window in the ODBC Data Source Administrator (Figure 12.3):

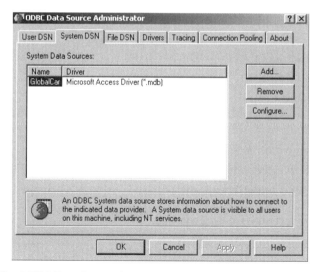

Figure 12.3 The ODBC Data Source Administrator.

If you are running Windows 95, 98 or NT – Go to **Start > Settings > Control Panel > ODBC > Select the System DSN tab**.

Or

If you are running Windows 2000 – Go to **Start > Settings > Control Panel > Administrative Tools > Data Sources (ODBC) > Select the System DSN tab**.

Or

If you are running Windows XP – Go to **Start > Control Panel > Administrative Tools > Data Sources (ODBC) > Select the System DSN tab**.

2. Click on the **Add** button to create a new connection.

3. Select the **Microsoft Access Driver** from the **Create New Data Source** window (Figure 12.4).

4. Click the **Finish** button.

5. In the set-up dialog box (Figure 12.5) enter a name for your database and a description of its contents (though the description is not essential).

6. Connect to your database by clicking the **Select** button.

7. Navigate to and select your database.

8. Click **OK** on that and all remaining ODBC windows to finish.

Connecting to your database

You've set up Dreamweaver to be able to process dynamic pages, now you need to tell it how to connect to your database.

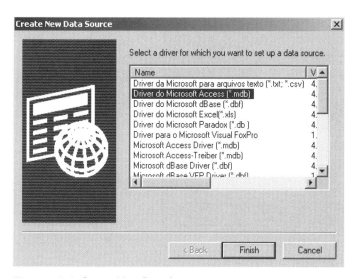

Figure 12.4   Create New Data Source window.

1. Open the **Databases** panel in the **Application panel** group (Figure 12.6).

2. Click on the plus (+) button and select **Data Source Name** to open the Connection window (Figure 12.7).

3. Type in a connection name.

4. Click on the DSN button to select the DSN we set up earlier (it may be set automatically).

5. Make sure the **Dreamweaver Should Connect: Using Local DSN** radio button is selected.

Figure 12.5 ODBC Microsoft Access Setup window.

Figure 12.6 The Databases panel.

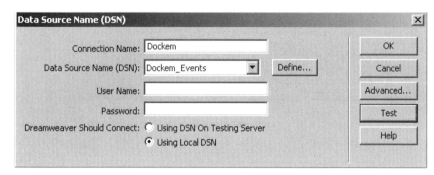

Figure 12.7 The Connection window.

6. Click on **Test** and you should see that the connection has been made successfully.

7. Click **OK**, and you should see the database in the **Database** panel.

OK … so we're ready to create the dynamic page.

Entering data fields in a page

The first thing you need to do is create an ASP page into which you are going to call up data. Go to **File > New >** under the **General** tab and select **Dynamic page and ASP VBScript**.

It is probably easiest to insert a table on the page and indicate with text where it is your data is going to display (Figure 12.8).

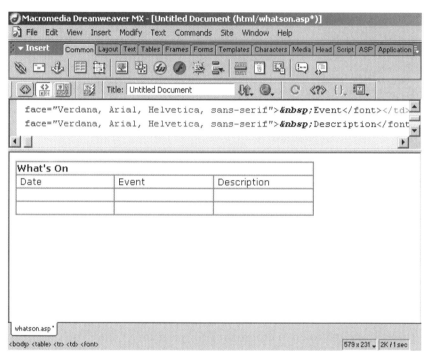

Figure 12.8 The What's On page.

Next, you need to create a recordset of the data we are going to use. To create a recordset:

Figure 12.9 The Bindings panel.

1. Open the **Bindings** panel in the **Application** panel group (Figure 12.9).

2. Click the (+) button and select **Recordset (Query)**.

3. In the **Recordset** window (Figure 12.10) give your recordset a name.

4. Select the connection you set up earlier and also select the table (database).

5. Click on the **Test** button to view your database records (Figure 12.11).

6. Click **OK** in both windows and your records should appear in the **Bindings** panel.

At last! You're ready to get that data to appear on your page!

1. In the ASP page you have set up, place the cursor where you want the data to appear.

2. In the **Bindings** panel, select the data category you want to appear, for example 'Events', and click the **Insert** button.

*Once you understand what's going on, you may prefer to use the **Insert Dynamic Table** option. Open the **Application** tab in the Insert bar and choose the **Insert Dynamic Table** button.*

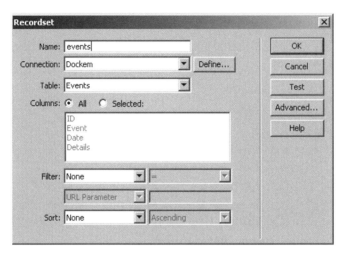

Figure 12.10 The Recordset window.

3. You should see a record placeholder appear in the page (Figure 12.12).

4. To get more than one record to appear you need to go to the **Server Behavior** panel, also found in the **Application** panel group.

5. Click on the (+) button and select **Repeat Region** from the drop-down menu.

6. In the **Repeat Region** window select your **Recordset** and choose how many records to display (Figure 12.13).

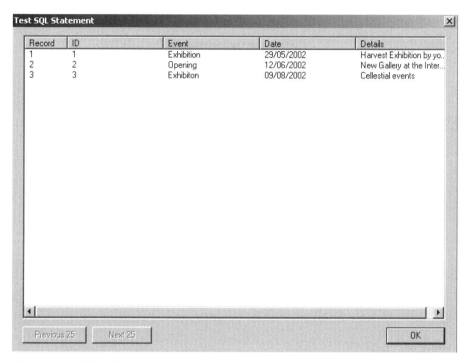

Test SQL Statement   [x]

Record	ID		Event	Date	Details
1	1		Exhibition	29/05/2002	Harvest Exhibition by yo...
2	2		Opening	12/06/2002	New Gallery at the Inter...
3	3		Exhibiton	09/08/2002	Cellestial events

Previous 25   Next 25   OK

Figure 12.11 Test SQL Statement window.

Try testing your page. You can test in the browser or in Dreamweaver by clicking on the **View Live Data** button on the toolbar. (Can't find it? Look back at Figure 2.4.) Pretty exciting stuff huh?

*You can set how you want date text to appear on the page. Go to the **Server Behaviors** panel and highlight the date dynamic text. Click on the (+) button and select **Dynamic text**. Select the date field and under Format choose the one you prefer.*

What's On		
Date	Event	Description
{events.Date}	{events.Event}	{events.Details}

Figure 12.12 A record placeholder.

Figure 12.13 The Repeat Region window.

You may need to set some permissions on your system to modify the database from a browser. To do so go to the Windows Explorer > Navigate to your site directory where the database is held > Right-click on database name and select Properties > Security tab > Add button > find the IUSR – machine name > Click add button > Click OK and in the permission settings check that Modify and Write are both selected.

Updating your database

The great thing about working with a dynamic site is that you can also add and delete records in your database from a Web browser.

Adding a record

You add records to a database by using an HTML form that holds the data and a server behaviour that processes it and sends it to the database. If you are a bit rusty with how to work with forms (or missed that chapter altogether) have a look at Chapter 7: Creating forms.

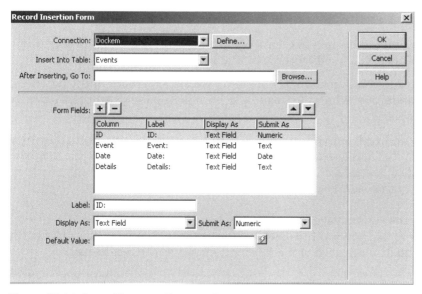

Figure 12.14 Record Insertion Form window.

It is very easy to set this up in Dreamweaver using an automated function (less fiddly and we like that).

1. Go to Insert > Application Objects > Record Insertion Form (Figure 12.14).

2. Complete the dialog box categories and click OK.

Make changes by either editing the form or clicking on the **Insert Record** behaviour in the **Server Behaviors** panel.

Deleting a record

So now you should be able to create pages that display database records and others that allow you to add records to that database.

The final thing you'll need to be able to do is delete a record in the database, for example in our What's On example, to delete gallery events that have already happened.

Deleting a record from your database is not quite as simple as displaying a record from it. There are quite a few steps involved which enable the database to be searched, the relevant records selected for deletion, and the deletion to be confirmed by the user.

Setting up the results page

To find the record you want to delete you need to create a page that links to the database and displays a list of records in it, known as the results page.

1. Create a page with a table and insert a text marker where your search results are going to be displayed (Figure 12.15).

2. Create a recordset of the data we are going to use. Go to the **Bindings** panel > Select the (+) button and choose **Recordset** from the drop-down menu > Select your connection and table and click **OK**.

3. In the HTML table you have set up, highlight the relevant text marker.

4. In the **Bindings** panel, select the data category you want to appear and click the **Insert** button (or drag the binding from the panel onto the page). Your table should now look something like Figure 12.16.

Date	Event	Description	Delete

Figure 12.15 Results page table set-up.

Date	Event	Description	
{Recordset1.EventDate}	{Recordset1.Event}	{Recordset1.Details}	Delete

Figure 12.16 Results page with bindings.

5. Create a blank delete page and save it as delete.asp.

6. In the results page highlight the **Delete** text in the table and in the **Property inspector** select the folder icon to make a link to the delete page you have just created.

7. Back in the **Select File** window select the **Parameters** button to open the **Parameters** dialog box (Figure 12.17.) Add a new parameter called ID and click on the lightning button to open the **Dynamic Data** window.

8. In the **Dynamic Data** window (Figure 12.18) select ID.

9. Click on **OK** twice to set the connection.

10. To display all of the records you need to set a **Repeat Region** server behaviour to the table row (just as we did in our original records display page). Highlight the table row. Go to the **Server Behaviors** panel > Click on the (+) button > Select **Repeat Region** from the drop-down menu.

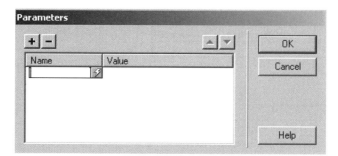

Figure 12.17 The Parameters dialog box.

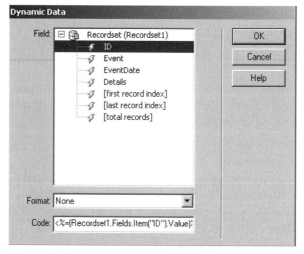

Figure 12.18 The Dynamic Data window.

Working with the delete page

The first thing you need for your delete page is to define a recordset for the deletions that includes a filter (which relates to the ID parameter we set up earlier).

1. Open your delete.asp page.

2. In the **Bindings** panel go to the (+) button and select **Recordset** from the drop-down menu.

3. Name the **Recordset** something like 'Remove'.

4. Use the same connection and table as before.

5. Go to the **Filter** drop-down menu and select **EventID**.

Next you need to type in some text on the page that confirms the deletion, then from the **Bindings** panel, insert the records you need to delete (Figure 12.19).

Confirm deletion

{Remove.ID} {Remove.Event} {Remove.EventDate} {Remove.Details}

Figure 12.19 Delete confirmation page.

You now need to add a Submit button to confirm the deletion.

1. Insert a Form Submit button at the bottom of the page and change the text of the button to something like 'OK – Delete record'.

Finally you need a server behaviour to the page to tell the database to delete the record.

1. Go to the **Server Behaviors** panel and click on the (+) button.

2. Select **Delete Record** from the drop-down menu.

3. In the **Delete Record** window (Figure 12.20) select your connection, table and check the other sections. Select a page for the user to return to after the deletion, such as the page where the database records are listed – in our example, the What's On page.

Figure 12.20 Delete Record window.

Some useful references

Access database tutorial at Stardeveloper.com: http://stardeveloper.com:8080/odbc_def.asp

Tips on building dynamic sites at the Ultradev Zone: www.udzone.com

Managing and publishing your site

13

Running a spellcheck

Testing the site

Last-minute cleaning-up

Inserting keywords and a description

Getting your site online

Setting up a remote site

Connecting to a remote server

Setting FTP preferences

Managing your site with Check In/Out

Using Design Notes

In this last chapter it's time to look at preparing the site for going 'live' and at getting the site online.

Running a spellcheck

It may sound obvious, but proofreading and spellchecking a site are the two most important tasks to do before putting anything online. While printed documents are usually proofread fastidiously (read backwards with one eye closed and all that), too often Web pages go live that are not really in a publishable state. It's probably easiest to print pages from the site and proofread them from paper, and better still to get someone unfamiliar with the content to do the proofing.

Remember that spellchecking is *not* the same as proofreading, and it is important to do both.

To run a spellcheck in Dreamweaver, go to **Text > Check Spelling**.

To select the language (UK or US English):

1. Go to **Edit > Preferences**.
2. In the **General** category select the language from the drop-down menu (Figure 13.1).

Testing the site

In Chapter 1 of this guide some reference was made to usability testing. It is something you may like to consider before publishing your site, and ideally early on in the development process. It doesn't need to be a long and expensive process and you only need a few people testing your site to pick up most of the

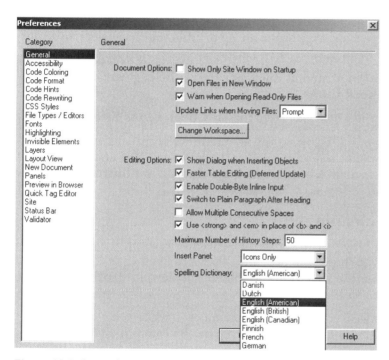

Figure 13.1 Setting language preferences.

major problems. For a light-hearted yet informative look at developing the user interface and testing you may enjoy reading Steve Krug's *Don't Make Me Think: A Common Sense Approach to Web Usability*, Circle.com Library, 2000.

If your site is very large it's probably a good idea to run a check to see if any links are broken (perhaps they are pointing to a file that has been moved outside Dreamweaver or to pages that no longer exist).

To check links within a current document: save the page and go to **File > Check Page > Check Links**.

To check links for the whole site: go to **Site > Check Links Sitewide**.

As a final part of your site testing you should preview the site in as many different browser versions as you can, on both platforms (Mac and PC). Even if you have a target audience, on a target platform, it never hurts to know how the site looks under different circumstances.

Last-minute cleaning-up

While you may or may not be very experienced at reading HTML, there are plenty of people out there who are, and it pays to keep your code clean and simple. It will also make your site work better and download faster if the code is as streamlined as possible.

Sometimes Dreamweaver puts in extra bits of code when you edit and re-edit pages, so it's a good idea to run a clean-up operation before you go live.

To run a clean-up:

1. Go to **Commands > Clean Up HTML** (Figure 13.2).
2. Make your choices from the options, but if you don't really know HTML leave the default options and click **OK**.

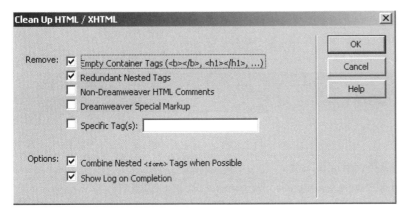

Figure 13.2 Clean-up HTML options.

Inserting keywords and a description

Keywords and descriptions are included in your page as <META> tags. Meta tags provide background information for a page in many different ways but keywords and descriptions are the most important and should generally be included on every page. Keywords let you list important words related to your site for search engines, and a description provides a summary of your site, or a particular page.

How to use keywords

It is crucial to include keywords on all of the pages in your site as many search engines use them to index your page. It is best to limit your keywords to about 20 words. While some engines may index more, the fewer the keywords, the more relevant each is considered to be by the search engine.

It's useful to make a list of your site keywords before you start building the site and then use them over and over in body text, image <ALT> tags and page titles. The more the words are used, the more chance they have of being noticed by a search engine!

To insert keywords:

1. From the **Insert** bar select the **Head** tab (Figure 13.3).

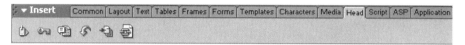

Figure 13.3 Meta tag options.

2. Choose the **Keywords** button.

3. Type in your keywords separated by commas (Figure 13.4).

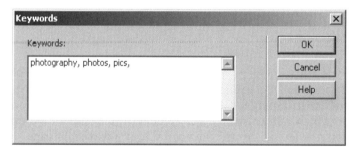

Figure 13.4 Inserting Keywords.

Creating a description

Your site description is what search engines display below the URL when your site comes up in a search. Some engines also use words in the description for their index. It is typical to write a one- or two-sentence site description, limiting it to about 15–20 words.

To insert your site description:

1. From the **Insert** bar select the **Head** tab.
2. Choose the **Description** button.
3. Type in your description (Figure 13.5).

Figure 13.5 Inserting a site description.

It's useful to keep a copy of your site description and keywords handy for when you submit your site to search engines. In many cases they will ask you to fill in description and keyword fields as part of the submission process.

To learn more about search engines and getting your site listed visit: www. searchenginewatch.com.

Getting your site online

The method for getting your site onto the Internet or uploading it to an Intranet is the same. In both cases you send files from a local site (the site you've been working on and testing) to a remote site which is the server 'hosting' the site and making it accessible on the Internet or on a company's Intranet.

When you upload your site to the Internet, all your files – HTML pages, images, Flash movies and other media – are sent, or 'uploaded', using FTP (File Transfer Protocol). You simply set up your FTP details (which will have been provided to you by whoever is hosting the site) in Dreamweaver and from within the Site Files window make the connection. You do need to have a modem, or access to the Internet, to make the FTP connection.

You generally do not need to use FTP to upload a site to a company Intranet – but check with the server administrator where the files should go.

Setting up a remote site

1. Go to **Site > Edit Sites**.

   Or

   Select **Edit Sites** from the site name drop-down menu in the Site window.

2. Highlight the site you want to define and click on **Edit**.

3. Choose **Remote Info** from the category list.

4. Choose FTP from the server Access drop-down menu (Figure 13.6). If you are uploading to an Intranet, choose **Local/Network** and use the folder to navigate to a directory where the site should go.

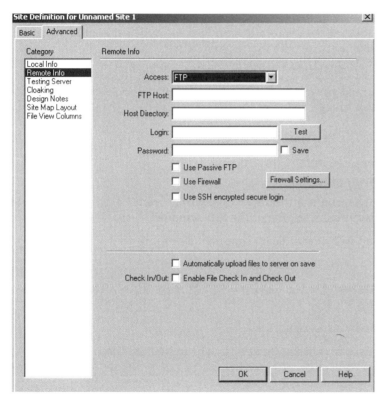

Figure 13.6 FTP options.

5. Fill in the field options with information provided by your Web host. The information requested here is totally standard so your host should provide it without a problem.

6. Click **OK** and then the **Done** button in the next dialog box.

Once you have defined your remote site profile the Connect, Get and Put buttons will be available along the top of the Site window.

Connecting to a remote server

1. Open the relevant site in the Site window.

2. Click on the **Connect** button.

3. The connection is made automatically and the remote site files should appear in the **Remote Site** area of the Site window.

The Connect button will now indicate that you are online.

To upload files:

- Highlight the file name in the local site and click the **Put** button.
  Or
- Drag the site file into the remote site.

You can drag and drop an entire site at a time or individual files.

To download files:

- Highlight the file name in the remote site and click the **Get** button.
  Or
- Drag the site file into the local site.

Setting FTP preferences

To change your FTP preferences, for example the site display and firewall settings:

1. Go to **Edit > Preferences**.
2. Select **Site** from the category list.
3. Make your changes in the FTP **Preferences** dialog box (Figure 13.7).

FTP options are:

- **Always Show**. Concerns the remote and local site display in the Site window.
- **Dependent Files**. Prompts you to upload or download dependent files on checking in or out (see next section).
- **FTP Connection**. The amount of time (minutes) Dreamweaver will maintain your connection after being idle. You may want to reduce this time if you are concerned about time online.
- **FTP Time Out**. The amount of time (seconds) that Dreamweaver will try to make a connection with the host (remote) server.
- **Firewall Host**. If you are working behind a firewall, type in the address of the proxy server.
- **Firewall Port**. Change if your connection port is one other than 21 (the default for FTP).
- **Put Options**. Fairly self-evident – save files before Putting (or uploading).

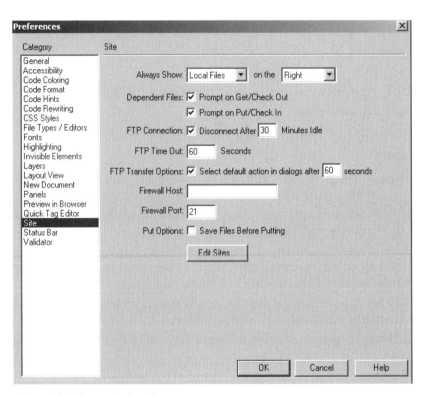

Figure 13.7 Setting FTP preferences.

Managing your site with Check In/Out

If you are working on a Website with a team of editors or writers, or with different people responsible for updating pages on a site, you may find the Dreamweaver Check In/Out facility useful. When you are editing pages you can 'check them out' of the site, thus preventing other people from editing them at the same time. You can also keep track of who last updated a file and when.

To enable the Check In/Out facility:

1. Go to **Site > Edit Sites**.
2. Highlight the site you want to set up and click on **Edit**.
3. Choose **Remote Info** from the category list.
4. Choose **FTP** or **Local/Network** from the server **Access** drop-down menu.
5. Select **Enable File Check In/Check Out** which will bring up the set-up options (Figure 13.8).
6. Type in a user name and an email address.

To check out a remote file:

1. Connect to the site in the Site window.
2. Highlight the file name (or multiple files) in the **Remote Site** and select the **Check Out** button along the top of the Site window.

   Or

   In the **Remote Site** double-click on a file.
3. Choose whether you want to download dependent files (such as images) with the file.

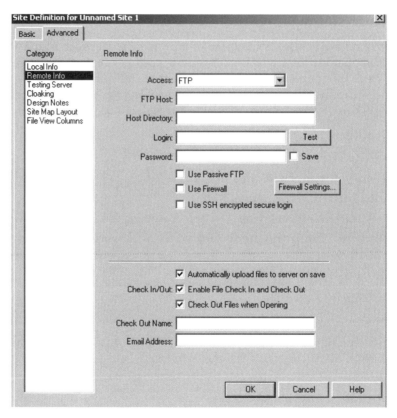

Figure 13.8 Check In/Check Out options.

To check in files:

1. Connect to the site in the Site window.
2. Highlight the file name (or multiple files) in the local site and select the **Check In** button along the top of the Site window.
3. Choose whether you want to upload dependent files.

Using Design Notes

Design Notes can enhance collaborative work by enabling you to share information with others on the team, or indeed make notes to yourself that are useful to have to hand. You can attach information to Web material you produce such as HTML pages, templates and images.

To set up general Design Notes for a page:

1. Go to **File > Design Notes** (Figure 13.9).
2. In the dialog box select the status of the file, add comments, use the calendar icon to insert the date and check the **Show When File Is Opened** box if appropriate.
3. Add other useful values in the **All Info** tab. To add a value you can name the value first in the name field then add the value in the value field, for instance **Name**=Designer, **Value**=Belinda, will display as Designer= Belinda (Figure 13.10).

Be aware that **Design Notes** *attached to a template are not passed on to pages created from that template.*

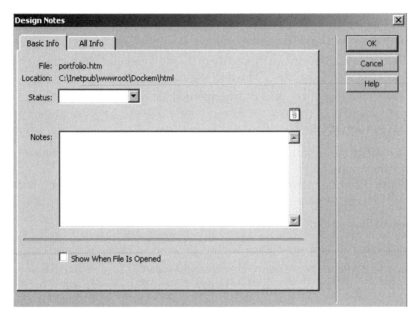

Figure 13.9 Design Notes – Basic Info.

To add Design Notes to an object:

1. Highlight the object, for example an image.
2. Right/Ctrl-click to access the **Context** menu.
3. Choose **Design Notes**.
4. Add the relevant notes.

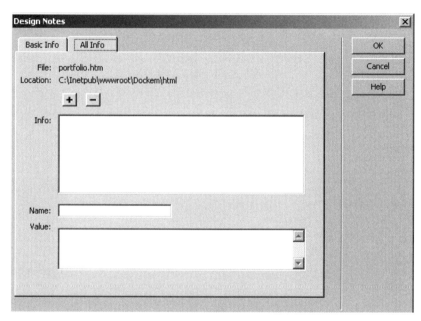

Figure 13.10 Design Notes – All Info.

Appendices

Appendix A – Naming files

Appendix B – The Web-safe Color Palette

Appendix C – Setting up and testing a Web server

Appendix A: Naming files

There are recognised and preferred file name conventions for the Web.

The first important file name to understand is that of your home page, or the first page that's to appear when someone calls for your Web address. A recognised home page name is 'index.html' and you shouldn't run into any problems if you use this (though index is not mandatory and you may be able to set up a different default home page file name with your host server). If you are running asp pages you should use the name default .html.

The extension of your file name is the bit that includes a dot and the letters after it, such as .htm or .html. Both of these extensions can be used for HTML files and it is essential to include them (files created within Dreamweaver will automatically be given the extension).

There are some other simple naming conventions that should help you avoid troubles once your site is online.

- Most importantly, avoid using spaces in your file or folder names such as 'pr may.htm' as this can cause real problems when uploaded to the server. Try using underscores to indicate a space such as 'pr_may.htm'.

- Avoid any special characters in your file names such as hyphens or exclamation marks and always start the name with a letter, not a number.

Appendix B: The Web-safe Color Palette

To accommodate users viewing the Web on a 256-colour screen, a limited selection of 216 colours, known as the Web-safe Color Palette, was defined as the colours common to Netscape Navigator and Microsoft Internet Explorer on both the Windows and Macintosh platforms. Even though Dreamweaver comes with the Web-safe palette as its default colour palette, you no longer need to stick to it as very few users are now working on a 256-colour screen.

Although much of what you read about Web-safe colour refers to the common colour palette consisting of 216 colours, Dreamweaver palettes display only 212 colours – those being the only colours properly supported by both platforms and browsers.

In HTML the colours are written in hexadecimal values for red, green and blue (RGB) and are a combination of the pairs 00, 33, 66, 99, CC or FF, preceded by a hash key (#). For example, white is written as #FFFFFF.

Appendix C: Setting up and testing a Web server

If you are using Windows and have been unable to locate a C:\Inetpub or a D:\Inetpub folder (which would indicate that you already have a Web server installed) then you need to install the server software on your system (don't panic … it's free!).

To install a Web server
There are a couple of options depending on your system.

If you use Windows 98 you should install PWS by accessing your Windows CD and going to the **Add-Ons > PWS** folder and following the instructions.

Better still, download the Windows NT option pack which includes IIS.4 and can run on Windows 95 and Windows 98 and NT Workstation.

If you are using NT Server, Windows 2000 or Windows XP you should install IIS by going to **Start > Settings > Control Panels > Add/Remove Programs**. Select **Add/Remove Windows Components** and select the IIS box to begin installation.

Once you have the software installed you should test whether it is working – that way you can have any server problems ironed out before tackling the Dreamweaver integration!

To test your server

1. Create a simple HTML page in Dreamweaver.

2. Name the page and save it in Inetpub\wwwroot\site_folder.

3. Open your browser and type in the address:

   http://localhost/site_folder/filename.html

If your page does not display you should first check that you have saved the file with the .html extension, and that you have typed the address correctly in the browser.

If that all seems OK go to the System tray and double-click the Web Server icon. In the Personal Web Manager window, click on the Start button if Web Publishing is turned off.

Index

A

A-Hover option, 125
<A> tag, 124
'A' toggle, 124
absolute links, 58
accented characters, 43
Access database, 171–4, 178
actions (in JavaScript), 148, 151–2
Active links, colour for, 38
alignment
    of images, 56–7
    of paragraphs, 41
    of tables, 80
Alt text, 10, 54
Always Show (FTP option), 201
anchor links, 60–2
animation of layers, 140–3
animation paths, 143
ASP (Active Server Pages), 171
Assets panel, 158, 166–8
Autoplay, 141
Autostretch (table cells), 75–7, 80

B

<B> tag (bold), 2
Back button, 141
background images and colour, 37

behaviours
    adding of, 155–6
    attached to objects, 148–51
    attached to timelines, 145–6
    commonly-used, 153
    deletion of, 152
    editing of, 151–2
Behaviours channel (in timeline), 141–2
<BLOCK-QUOTE> tag, 41
bold text, 2, 40
borders
    around frames, 94
    around images, 59
    around tables, 80
browsers, 2
    compatibility of, 130, 140
    preferences for, 48–9
    speech-synthesised, 10, 41, 54
bullet-point lists, 44
buttons in forms, 103–4, 112

C

cells (in tables)
    adding content to, 73
    autostretch, 75–7, 80
    drawing of, 71–3
    formatting of, 81–2
    layout of, 74–5

    merging and splitting of, 84
    width of, 75–7
CGI (Common Gateway Interface), 100
Check Browser behaviour, 153
Check In/Out facility, 203–5
Check Plugin behaviour, 153
checkboxes (in forms), 103, 106
clip options, 134–5
Code and Design view, 17
Code view, 17
colour
    for links, 38
    of text, 40
colour schemes, 36
columns (in tables)
    adding and deleting of, 83
    formatting of, 82–3
    width of, 75
compression of files, 52
contents page, 89
context menus, 23–4
creation of files and folders, 28
CSS (Cascading Style Sheets), 34, 116, 119–27
CSS Selector, 121, 124
Custom styles, 119, 121
    creation and application of, 122–3
    removal and redefinition of, 123–4
customisation of workspace, 23

D

database-driven Websites, 9
databases
    adding records to, 184–5
    connecting Dreamweaver to, 176–9
    deletion of records in, 186–90
    entering data fields in a page, 179–84
    set-up, 173–4
    updating of, 184
    working with, 171–2
Dependent Files (FTP option), 201
descriptions of Websites, 195, 197
Design Notes, 205–7
Design view, 14, 17
dictionary, 47
<DIV> tag, 134
Document window, 14
domain names, 3
download time, 19
downloadable text, 8
DSN (Data Source Name), 172
    creation of, 175–6
dummy links, 150
Dynamic HTML, 9, 130, 140
dynamic Websites, 9

E

Edit Font List window, 40
editable regions in templates, 161–2
email links, 59–60
Enctype, 101–2
events in JavaScript, 148
Extension Manager, 153, 155–6
external style sheets, 121, 125–7
Eyedropper tool, 37

F

F-keys, xx, 20
Favorites, 168
file fields (in forms), 110–11
file management, 9–11, 25
file name extensions, 210
file names, 37, 210
files, creation and deletion of, 28
Firewall Host and Firewall Port (FTP options),
    201
fixed window layout, 14–15
floating window layout, 14, 16
folders, 10, 25
    creation of, 28
    deletion of, 28–9
font selection, 38–40
form objects, 103–12
formatting
    of framesets, 92–3
    of individual frames, 93–5
    of table cells, rows and columns, 81–3
    of text, 38–9
forms, 100
    buttons on, 103–4, 112; *see also* radio
        buttons
    creation of, 101
    handling methods, 101
    submission of data on, 100
<FORM> tag, 101
Forward button, 141
Fps (frames per second) setting, 141
frame numbers (for animations), 142
frame pages
    adding content to, 91
    saving of, 92

<FRAME> tag, 92
frames, 88–9
    borders and margins of, 94
    formatting of, 93–5
    naming of, 94
    width and height of, 93
frameset page, 89
<FRAMESET> tag, 92
framesets
    creation of, 89–91
    formatting of, 92–3
    nested, 96
    properties of, 92–3
    saving of, 92
FTP (File Transfer Protocol), 4, 198–9
    set-up of preferences, 201–2

G

GET method (for handling forms), 101
GIF format, 52
'Go' button (in forms), 64
'Go to URL' behaviour, 153
graphics, 8
    users' views of, 10
graphics programs, 55

H

headings, creation of, 38
hidden fields (in forms), 103, 111
hidden layers, 144
home page, 11, 30, 46, 210
horizontal rules, 42–3
host servers, 3–4, 198
hotspots on image maps, 65–7
<HR> tag, 42–3

HREF (Hypertext Reference) attribute, 57
HTML (Hypertext Markup Language), 2–3, 17
HTML styles, 116–19
HTML tags, 2, 19
    clean-up of, 45–6, 194–5
    redefinition of, 121
    styles converted to, 126
    see also Dynamic HTML
hyperlinks, 2
    creation of, 57–62

I

image editing programs, 55
image fields, 112
image maps, 55, 65–7
images, 8
    alignment of, 56–7
    borders for, 59
    duplication of, 52
    insertion of, 52
    properties of, 52–6
    resizing of, 56
    turned off by Website users, 10, 54
import into Dreamweaver
    of tables, 85–6
    of text, 45–6
index.html files, 11, 46, 210
indexing of Websites, 8, 195
Insert bar, 20–1
installation of Dreamweaver MX, xix
interactive forms, 100
Internet, the, 4, 171
    uploading to, 3, 198
Internet Explorer, 2
Internet Information Server, 172

Intranets, 198
Invisible Elements, 62, 131–2
italic text, 40

J

JavaScript, 52, 148, 153
JPEG format, 52
jump menus, 62–5, 153

K

keyframes, 142, 144–5
keywords, 8, 195–7

L

Launcher bar, 19
layers, 71
    animation of, 140
    conversion into tables, 140
    creation of, 130–2
    hidden, 144
    nested, 133, 136–7
    preferences for, 138–9
    properties of, 132–5
    working with, 135–8
Layout view, 71–2
layout for Web pages, 70
Library items, 158, 164–6
line breaks, 41–2
linking *see* hyperlinks
    between pages in a frameset, 95–6
    using image maps, 65–7
    using jump menus, 62–5
lists
    numbered or bulleted, 44
    for user choice, 104, 109–10

Live Data view, 18
local sites, 25, 173
looping (in animation), 141, 146

M

Macintosh computers, running Dreamweaver
    MX with, xix–xxi, 134
Macromedia, xviii
margins for frames, 95
menus
    for user choice, 104, 109
    see also jump menus
merging of cells, 84
<META> tag, 21, 195
Microsoft *see* Internet Explorer; MIDAC;
    Windows; Word
MIDAC (Microsoft Data Access components),
    175
mouse rollovers, 52, 67, 148, 151, 154

N

named anchors, 60–2
navigation around Websites, 7
navigation page, 89
nested framesets, 96
nested layers, 133, 136–7
nested tables, 77–8
Netscape Navigator, 2, 134, 139
No Resize option, 94
NoFrames content, 98
non-breaking spaces, 44
None button, 104
numbered lists, 44

O

objects in JavaScript, 148
<OL> tag, 44
Open Browser Window behaviour, 153
opening a Web page, 34–5
opening a Website, 29
overflow options for layers, 134
overlapping layers, 133, 137

P

<P> tag, 41
Page Layout, 73
Page properties, 36–8
page size, 19
page titles, 37
panel groups, 22–3
panel shortcuts, xx–xxi, 20
paragraph alignment, 41
paragraph breaks, 41
password fields (in forms), 105
PDF (Portable Document Format) files, 7
permission settings, 184
personal computers, use of Dreamweaver with, xix–xx
Personal Web Server, 172
photographic images, 52
placeholders, 53
Play Sound option, 154
popup messages, 154
POST method (for handling forms), 101
Preload Images behaviour, 154
Prevent Overlaps box, 137
previewing of Websites, 47–8, 194
printing
    of pages, 48–9
    of Site Map, 31

proofreading a site, 192
Property inspector, 20, 38, 56
Put Options (for FTP), 201

R

radio buttons (in forms), 103, 107–8
records
    added to databases, 184–5
    deleted from databases, 186–90
relative links, 58
remote sites, set-up of, 198–200
Reset button (on a form), 104
resize handles, 76, 80
resizing
    of images, 56
    of tables, 85
rollover images, 67
rollovers *see* mouse rollovers
rows
    adding and deleting of, 83
    formatting of, 82–3

S

saving
    as HTML, 45, 86
    of pages, 46–7
    Save All Frames option, 92
scrolling, 94
search engines, 8, 37, 89, 195, 197
servers, 170–1; *see also* host servers; Web servers
'Set Text of Status Bar' behaviour, 154
shortcuts *see* panel shortcuts
'Show/Hide Layers' behaviour, 154
site cache, 27
Site definition window, 25–6

Site Files window, 27
site folder, 25, 34
Site list, using Assets from, 167
Site map, 30–1
Site window, 29, 35, 47
spacer images, 77
<SPAN> tag, 121, 134
spanning columns (in tables), 84
special characters, 43–4
spellchecking, 47, 192
split screen option, 17
splitting of cells (in tables), 84
stacking order of layers, 133, 138
Standard view, 71
    tables created in, 79–85
'static' Web pages, 9
Status bar, 19
style sheets *see* CSS
styles, 34, 116–19
    conflict between, 119
    editing of, 125
Submit button, 104
Swap Image behaviour, 154
system requirements for Dreamweaver MX, xviii–xix

T

table layout options, 74
<TABLE> tag, 70
tables, 70–1
    alignment of, 80
    borders for, 80
    converted from layers, 140
    created in Standard view, 79–85
    imported into Dreamweaver, 85–6
    nested, 77–8
    pre-set layouts for, 85

properties of, 80
resizing, 85
tags *see* HTML tags
<TD> tag, 70
templates
    attachment of existing pages to, 162–3
    creation of, 158–60
    creation of new pages from, 162
    detaching pages from, 163
    editable regions in, 161–2
    preferences for, 163
testing
    of Web servers, 212
    of Websites, 2, 7, 80, 192–4
testing servers, set-up of, 173–4
text
    colour of, 40
    creation and formatting of, 38–40
    import of, 45–6
    size of, 40
text fields (in forms), 103–5
thumbnails, 8
timelines, 23, 140–2
    and animation, 142–3
    adding behaviours to, 145–6

editing layers in, 144
modification of, 144–5
multiple, 146
options for behaviours, 154–5
Toolbar, 18
<TR> tag, 70

U
<UL> tag, 44
Ultradev, 170
uploading to a host server, 3, 198
URLs (uniform resource locators), 3, 60

V
validation of forms and fields, 154
view options in Dreamweaver, 14, 17–18
visibility (Vis) settings for layers, 134, 138
Visited links, colour for, 38
voice browsers, 10, 41

W
Web-safe Color Palette, 210–11
Web servers, 172
    installation of, 211–12

testing of, 212
Websites, 2
    creation of, 3
    dynamic, 9
    goals of, 5–6
    management of, 9–10
    planning of, 5–7
    set-up, 24–7
    target audiences for, 6–7
'widgets', 103
width of cells and columns (in tables), 75–7
width of frames, 93
window layouts, fixed and floating, 14–15
Windows, running Dreamweaver MX with, xix,
    xxi
Word, 86
    import of text from, 45–6
'Working documents' folder, 25
workspace
    customization of, 23
    selection of, 14

Z
Z-index, 133, 138